FRONT SIGHT PRESENTS

CONSTITUTIONAL

DEFENSE

OF YOUR

Family

&

Freedom

WORKBOOK

Constitutional Defense

For additional copies of this workbook or for more information on other books, contact:

Revolutionary Strategies
P.O. Box 900
Dripping Springs, TX 78620
(512)515-3744
www.RickGreen.com

Cover & Disc design:
Daniel Hook

Printed in the United States of America
ISBN 978-0-9981269-3-7

DEDICATION

Dr. Ignatius Piazza

*For having the vision, passion, and persistence to create
the most effective, most successful firearms training facility
in the history of the Second Amendment!*

America's Founding Fathers

*You launched the most successful nation in history. May our
generation honor your wisdom and sacrifice by preserving the
Torch of Freedom for future generations.*

WORKBOOK CONTENTS

ACKNOWLEDGMENTS

Though an attorney (please do not hold that against me!) and former Texas State Representative involved in defending our founding principles for twenty years, I am not in any way claiming to be a Constitutional guru. I am not, by a long shot, the foremost expert on the *Constitution*. In fact, I am just like you. I am a citizen that is learning as I go.

One of the great benefits of co-hosting *"WallBuilders Live! with David Barton and Rick Green"* is the privilege of always learning new things about the Constitution and pieces of history that helped me to better understand the document.

I have the privilege of working with someone who *is* one of the foremost experts on the Founding Fathers and our Founding Documents, David Barton. Through my work as host of WallBuilders Live!, I also get to interview and spend time with some of the greatest legal and constitutional minds of our day. Mat Staver, Kelly Shackleford, Brad Dacus, Ed Meece, John Eidsmoe, Newt Gingrich, Mike Farris, Congressman Louis Gohmert, and so many others. We also work with some amazing individuals who have been responsible for re-igniting interest in our founding documents: Glenn Beck, Dennis Prager, Rabbi Daniel Lapin, Bob McEwen, Gen. Jerry Boykin, Chuck Norris, and more great Americans than we have space to list here. It is from these individuals that I almost daily discover new golden nuggets of information that send me back to the writings of the Founding Fathers for more understanding about the greatest government documents ever conceived in history.

I include all of that information to simply say that you do not need to be an attorney or professor or any other kind of "expert" to study the *Constitution* and understand the principles of America. In this class, we will discover the admonishment of America's Founders for *"every citizen,"* regardless of background, education, or position, to read and study the *Constitution*. The very purpose of this book is to give all of us the tools to do that. We are in this together, so together let us study and learn and improve.

To David Barton, forgive me for being repetitive, but the same words apply even more today than when I wrote *Freedom's Frame*. You live more like Christ than any other man I have ever known. Thank you for your example, your mentorship, and your friendship. Like many others, I am taking a leisurely stroll down a path that you labored long and hard to blaze. Generations are indebted to you for the role you have played in preserving our nation's heritage.

To the Torch of Freedom Foundation Board and supporters, thanks for investing in the next generation.

To Mom and Dad, thank you for instilling a love of America and Her principles.

To my Sovereign Lord and Savior, Jesus Christ, thank you for the most important freedom of all.

To my wife Kara, thank you for accepting the calling the Lord has put on our lives. No matter how many twists and turns, victories and defeats, highs and lows, you continue to be the most amazing, steadfast partner I could ever have dreamed I would have.

To Mike Holler for creating the Constitution Made Easy.

To Dr. Ignatius Piazza, thank you for creating a place where my family could learn to defend ourselves. You have done more to change the image of gun ownership than anyone in the Nation. Thank you for your tireless efforts.

To the Front Sight Executive Team, instructors, and staff, thank you for running a smooth and effective operation. Thank you for the expert training you provide and for making it fun during the process!

PREFACE

This Classroom Workbook is your easy to use note taking tool during the classroom presentation of ***CONSTITUTIONAL DEFENSE!***

If you are attending the abbreviated version of the course, there will be many blanks or sections left uncovered...think of that part as homework! All of the answers are found in the back of this workbook and more detail can be found by watching the full DVD version. Some questions and answers are purposefully not covered in the DVD's so that you can enjoy the process of your own hunt for national treasures!

EPISODE ONE
Why We Train

The best way to honor those who gave their one life for our freedom is to _____[1] the freedom for which they sacrificed.

> *"The right of self-defense is the first law of nature; in most governments, it has been the study of rulers to confine this right within the narrowest limits possible. "Wherever the right of the people to keep and bear arms is prohibited under any color or pretext whatsoever, liberty, if not already annihilated, is on the brink of destruction."* **– St. George Tucker**
> **Revolution Soldier, Federal Judge, & Law Professor**

The law of self-defense is often called "the ____ ____[2] of nature."

"[T]o preserve liberty, it is essential that the whole body of the people always possess arms, and be taught alike, especially when young, how to use them…"

– Richard Henry Lee, Declaration Signer

While the Second Amendment protects our right to keep and bear arms, it is our job to protect the Second Amendment through our activity as citizens.

With every right, there is a _____[3].

In order to prevent an erosion of liberty, we must study the _____[4] of that liberty.

Constitutional Defense gives you the _____ _____[5] to defend and assert your rights.

The "_____[6]" in the founding era was every man that could fire a rifle, so the 2nd Amendment was not for the official military, but rather for "____ _____ _____[7]."

Original proposals for the Bill of Rights give us insight into what the Founders meant for the 2nd Amendment:

New Hampshire proposed the following language:

Congress shall never disarm any citizen.[i]

At the **Massachusetts** Convention, wording had been proposed declaring:

[T]hat the said Constitution be never construed . . . to prevent the people of the United States, who are peaceable citizens, from keeping their own arms.[ii]

Judge Zephaniah Swift authored the _____ _____ _____ [8] in America.

"Self-defense, or self-preservation, is one of the first laws of nature, which no man ever resigned upon entering society."

– Judge Zephaniah Swift

James Kent and Joseph Story laid the foundation for _____ _____[9].

> *"The municipal law of our country has likewise left with individuals the exercise of the natural right of self-defense. The right of self-defense is founded in the law of nature and is not — and cannot be — superseded by the law of society."*
>
> **– James Kent**

> *"The right of the citizens to keep and bear arms has justly been considered as the palladium of the liberties of a republic since it offers a strong moral check against the usurpation and arbitrary power of rulers and will enable the people to triumph over them. There is certainly no small danger that indifference may lead to disgust, and disgust to contempt, and thus gradually undermine all the protection intended by this clause of our national Bill of Rights."*
>
> **– Joseph Story, original Supreme Court Justice**

"Forty years ago when the resolution of enslaving America was formed in Great Britain, the British Parliament was advised to disarm the people; - that it was the best and most effectual way to enslave them – but that they should not do it openly, but to weaken them and let them sink gradually."

– George Mason, father of the Bill of Rights

The right to join together and form a militia for collective self-defense comes from our _____ _____[10] to self-defense.

"The Constitution should never be construed to prevent the people of the United States who are peaceable citizens from keeping their own arms."

– Samuel Adams, Declaration signer

"The advantage of being armed is an advantage which the Americans possess over the people of almost every other nation. In the several kingdoms of Europe, the governments are afraid to trust the people with arms."

– James Madison, father of the Constitution

"No citizen shall be debarred the use of arms within his own lands."

– Thomas Jefferson

"Resistance to sudden violence for the preservation not only of my person, my limbs, and life, but of my property, is an indisputable right of nature which I never surrendered to the public by the compact of society and which, perhaps, I could not surrender if I would.... [T]he maxims of the law and the precepts of Christianity are precisely coincident in relation to this subject."[iii]

– John Adams, U.S. President, Signer of The Declaration, One of The Two Signers of The Bill of Rights

"The Supreme Being gave existence to man, together with the means of preserving that existence. He invested man with an inviolable right to personal liberty and personal safety."

– Alexander Hamilton

_____ _____[11] signed the Declaration and the Constitution, was the 2nd most active member of the Constitutional Convention, and served on the first Supreme Court.

> "The great natural law of self-preservation cannot be repealed or superseded or suspended by any human institution. The right of the citizens to bear arms in the defense of themselves shall not be questioned.
>
> "Every man's house is deemed by the law to be his castle; and the law invests him with the power and places on him the duty of the commanding officer of his house. Every man's house is his castle, and if anyone be robbed in it, it shall be esteemed his own default and negligence."
>
> **– James Wilson**

THE FATE OF THE FREE WORLD DEPENDS UPON _____[12]!

EPISODE ONE TAKE AWAYS:

1. The right of self-defense is a law of nature, not something given to us by government...it is to be *protected* by government.

2. We each have a responsibility as a citizen to study the foundations of liberty and our Constitution so that we can peaceably protect, defend and assert our rights.

_____

_____

_____

_____

_____

_____

_____

_____

_____

_____

EPISODE TWO
WHY WE FIGHT

"As I have traveled across the country, I have been astounded just how many of our fellow citizens feel strongly about their constitutional rights but have no idea what they are, or for that matter, what the Constitution says. I am not suggesting that they become Constitutional scholars -- whatever that means. I am suggesting, however, that if one feels strongly about his or her rights, it does make sense to know generally what the Constitution says about them. It is at least as easy to understand as a cell phone contract -- and vastly more important."[iv]

– Clarence Thomas, U.S. Supreme Court Justice

There is something happening in America!

More than ever in my lifetime, people are hungry for knowledge and truth. They are searching out the formula of our freedom, seeking the principles that somehow made America the most successful nation in the history of the world. They are digging deep and they refuse to accept shallow answers while they demand that we return to our roots.

As we journey back to Independence Hall, we may not find the fictional Benjamin Franklin glasses to decode a secret message on the back of the Declaration of Independence (from the movie *National Treasures*); but we will most certainly re-discover on the front side of our founding documents the secret sauce of American Exceptionalism.

The founding principles, our freedom formula, is in plain language and their restoration simply requires us to read them and then stand up for them.

****

It is important to spend time in the past because history shows us the _____[1] that has made us the most successful nation in history up to this point.

"No free government, nor the blessings of liberty, can be preserved to any people but by a _____ _____[2] to fundamental principles."

– George Mason

The Constitution still works today, even two centuries later, because it was based on timeless principles of jurisdiction that govern human behavior.

Most of the Signers of the *Declaration of Independence* signed the document on _____[3]. When they signed, many of them believed it would be their _____ _____[4].

At the age of only 21, Captain _____ _____[5] was captured after volunteering for a recon mission. Just before he was hung, he gave a passionate speech for freedom and closed with his famous "one life" statement that has inspired generations to sacrifice for freedom.

Abraham Lincoln said we should take "_____

_____[6] *to the cause for which they gave the last full measure of devotion.*"[v]

All of us can help prepare the next generation by getting our local school districts to participate in _____ _____ _____[7]. (visit RickGreen.com and click on your state to see how you can help.)

It is time for us to heed the challenge of our very first **Chief Justice of the U.S. Supreme Court, John Jay:**

"Every member of the State ought diligently to read and to study the constitution of his country, and teach the rising generation to be free. By _____ their rights, they will sooner _____ when they are violated, and be the better prepared to _____ and _____[8] them."[vi]

This quote by one of the authors of *The Federalist Papers* sums up the purpose of this class and provides the outline of our journey together through our founding documents.

Our Approach

1. This is not an exhaustive study.

Think of this Constitutional Defense class as the "_____ _____ _____[9]" to the Constitution, so that we as citizens can get plugged in. Then, you should go back home and study the Constitution more extensively.

Recommended resources for further study:

o   Hillsdale College's Constitution program

o   National Center for Constitutional Studies' program

o   *The 5,000-Year Leap* by W. Cleon Skousen

o   *The Heritage Guide to the Constitution* by Edwin Meese, Dr. Matthew Spalding, and Dr. David Forte

Our goal is to _____ our rights, and know how to _____ and _____[10] them.

2. Focus on _____ _____[11], not judicial interpretation.

"On every question of construction, carry ourselves back to the time when the Constitution was adopted, recollect the spirit manifested in the debates, and instead of trying what meaning may be squeezed out of the text, or invented against it, conform to the probable one in which it was passed."[vii]

– Thomas Jefferson

"I entirely concur in the propriety of resorting to the sense in which the Constitution was accepted and ratified by the nation. In that sense alone it is the legitimate Constitution. And if that be not the guide in expounding it, there can be no security for a consistent and stable [constitution], more than for a faithful, exercise of its powers.

"What a metamorphosis would be produced in the code of law if all its ancient phraseology were to be taken in its modern sense."

– James Madison

"The first and governing maxim in the interpretation of a statute is to discover the meaning of those who made it."

– James Wilson

"The first and fundamental rule in the interpretation of all documents is to construe them according to the sense of the terms and the intentions of the parties."[viii]

– Joseph Story

Original Intent is like the "owner's manual" of the Constitution: it helps us identify the correct application of the tools we have been given.

Once we understand the original meaning, the _____[12] that is communicated is the same and completely applicable to today.

3. Take sections as _____[13].

4. Use plain language for basic understanding, but not as a substitute for the _____ _____[14].

In the latter half of your workbook you will find *The Constitution Made Easy* by Michael Holler. This has the original text on the left and the plain-language amended version on the right.

We have a responsibility to teach the Constitution, not just to the rising generation, but to _____[15] around us. In our day of social media, everyone has a _____[16].

You do not have to have a lot of academic credentials to understand the Constitution. The founding fathers were ordinary men, and the Constitution they made was for ordinary people.

When studying the Constitution, it is important to start with the *Declaration of Independence* because the Constitution is the _____ of the _____[17] set forth in the *Declaration.*

There is a movement to _____[18] the Declaration from the Constitution, because if we the people ignore the principles behind it, politicians can distort the actual wording.

"[T]he virtue which had been infused into the Constitution of the United States ... was no other than the concretion of those abstract principles which had been first proclaimed in the Declaration of Independence.... **This was the platform upon which the Constitution of the United States had been erected.** *Its virtues, its republican character, consisted in its conformity to the principles proclaimed in the Declaration of Independence and as its administration ... was to depend upon the ... virtue, or in other words, of those principles proclaimed in the Declaration of Independence and embodied in the Constitution of the United States."[ix]*

– John Quincy Adams, at "The Jubilee of the Constitution"

In business terms, the Declaration of Independence is like the _____ of _____[19], telling who we are and what we are about, and the Constitution is like the _____[20], telling how the business will operation.

"Before the formation of the Constitution, the Declaration was received and ratified by all the States in the Union and has _____ [21] been disannulled."[x]

– Samuel Adams, Father of the American Revolution

"[The Constitution] is but the body and the letter of which the former is the thought and the spirit, and it is always safe to read the letter of the constitution in the spirit of the Declaration of Independence."[xi]

– U.S. Supreme Court

On June 7, 1776, _____ _____ _____ [22] from Virginia made the following motion for our independence, and was seconded by John Adams:

"Resolved, that these united colonies are and of right ought to be free and independent states. That they are absolved from all allegiance to the British crown and that all political connection between them and the rule of Great Britain ought to be totally dissolved."[xii]

The members of the committee appointed on June 11th to draft the *Declaration of Independence*xiii consisted of:

1.   Thomas Jefferson

2.   _____

3.   _____

4.   _____

5.   _____ 23

_____

_____

_____

_____

Which three states voted against Independence on July 1, 1776?

1. _____

2. _____

3. _____ _____ 24

_____ _____[25] made the midnight 80-mile horseback ride to reach Philadelphia just in time to cast the tie-breaking vote for Delaware to support independence when the vote was taken again.

The Framers' Formula for Lasting Freedom

*"We hold these **truths to be self-evident**: that all men are created equal, that they are **endowed by their Creator** with certain unalienable rights, that among these are life, liberty, and the **pursuit of happiness**; that to secure these rights, governments are instituted among men, deriving their just powers from the **consent of the governed**..."[xiv]*

The Declaration of Independence includes four essential principles that hold our freedom firmly in place:

1. _____[26] (The undeniable fact that moral absolutes exist.)

2. _____[27] (Our unalienable right to individual freedom comes from God)

3. _____[28] (We have a voice
in our government.)

4. _____[29] (The importance
of free enterprise to our freedom.)

Self-evident Truths & Endowed by Our Creator

"Of all the dispositions and habits which lead to political prosperity, religion and morality are indispensable supports. In vain would that man claim the tribute of patriotism, who should labor to subvert these great pillars of human happiness.... The mere politician, equally with the pious man, ought to respect and to cherish them."[xv]

– George Washington

The American Revolution was _____ _____
_____[30] and it led to the most successful nation in the history of the world. The French Revolution was

_____ _____ _____[31] and it led to the guillotine and total chaos.

The normal model of government in 1776 was based on the idea that power flowed from _____ to the _____ to the _____[32]. The American model reversed the last two so that power flows from _____[33] directly to _____[34] and then power is given to _____[35] only as the people deem appropriate.

If government does not _____[36] us our freedom, then government cannot rightfully _____[37] it away.

Thomas Jefferson even noted that the firm _____ ___ _____[38] was for people to remember that liberty is a gift from God.[xvi]

When delegates to the Constitutional Convention began to despair, _____[39] Franklin, the elder statesman, spoke on June 28, 1787, in an attempt to get the delegates back on track:

"Mr. President, the small progress we have made after four or five weeks close attendance & continual reasonings with each other—our different sentiments on almost every question, several of the last producing as many noes and ays, is methinks a melancholy proof of the imperfection of the Human Understanding. We indeed seem to feel our own want of political wisdom, since we have been running about in search of it. We have gone back to ancient history for models of Government, and examined the different forms of those Republics which having been formed with the seeds of their own dissolution now no longer exist. And we have viewed Modern States all round Europe, but find none of their Constitutions suitable to our circumstances.

"In this situation of this Assembly, groping as it were in the dark to find political truth, and scarce able to distinguish it when presented to us, how has it happened, Sir, that we have not hitherto once thought of humbly applying to the Father of lights to illuminate our understandings?

In the beginning of the contest with Great Britain, when we were sensible to danger, we had daily prayer in this room for Divine protection. Our prayers, Sir, were heard, and they were graciously answered. All of us who were engaged in the struggle must have observed frequent instances of a superintending Providence in our favor… [H]ave we now forgotten that powerful Friend? Or do we imagine we no longer need His assistance? I have lived, Sir, a long time, and the longer I live, the more convincing proofs I see of this truth—that God Governs in the affairs of men. And if a sparrow cannot fall to the ground without His notice, is it probable that an empire can rise without His aid?

We have been assured, Sir, in the Sacred Writing, that 'except the Lord build the House, they labor in vain that build it.' I firmly believe this; and I also believe that without His concurring aid we shall succeed in this political building no better than the builders of Babel…

I therefore beg leave to move—that henceforth prayers imploring the assistance of Heaven, and its blessing on our deliberations, be held in this Assembly every morning before we proceed to business…" xvii

– Benjamin Franklin, Declaration and Constitution Signer

"The real wonder is that the Constitutional Convention overcame so many difficulties. And to overcome them with so much agreement was as unprecedented as it was unexpected. It is impossible for the pious man not to recognize in it a finger of that Almighty Hand which was so frequently extended to us in the critical stages of the Revolution." xviii

– James Madison, Father of the Constitution

"For my own part, I sincerely esteem a system which, without the finger of God, never could have been suggested and agreed upon by such a diversity of interests."[xix]

– Alexander Hamilton, Constitution Signer & co-author of the Federalist Papers

"As to my sentiments with respect to the new Constitution, it appears to me little short of a miracle. It demonstrates as visibly the finger of Providence as any possible event in the course of human affairs can ever designate it."[xx]

– George Washington, Constitution Signer & Presiding Officer of the Convention

The Pursuit of Happiness

"A wise and frugal government, which shall leave men free to regulate their own pursuits of industry and improvement, and shall not take from the mouth of labor bread it has earned - this is the sum of good government."[xxi]

– Thomas Jefferson

William Bradford and the Pilgrims tried socialism, which Governor Bradford said caused much "_____ and _____[40], *and retard[ed] much employment, that would have been to their benefit, and comfort"*[xxii] and caused people to *"allege weakness and inability."*

After starving literally to death (many of them), Bradford made two very important changes by implementing _____ _____ and _____ _____[41].

They were soon exporting corn and thriving.

"This had very good success; for it made all hands very industrious, so as much more corn was planted, than otherwise would have been; by any means the Governor or any other could use, and saved him a great deal of trouble, and gave far better content." [xxiii]

– Gov. William Bradford

NOTE: Remember these things when we get to the Commerce Clause in Article 1, Section 8!

Consent of the Governed

According to President James Garfield, who is to blame when we have a Congress that is out of control and foolish? _____ [42]

"Now, more than ever before, the people are responsible for the character of their Congress. If that body be ignorant, reckless, and corrupt, it is because the people tolerate ignorance, recklessness, and corruption. If it be intelligent, brave, and pure, it is because the people demand these high qualities to represent them in the national legislature.... If the next centennial does not find us a great nation ... it will be because those who represent the enterprise, the culture, and the morality of the nation do not aid in controlling the political forces.''[xxiv]

– President James Garfield

"Controlling the political forces" simply means _____ or _____ [43] our consent.

"It is a great mistake to suppose that the paper we are to propose will govern the United States. It is the men whom it will bring into the Government and interest in maintaining it that is to govern them. The paper will only mark out the mode and the form. Men are the substance and must do the business.''[xxv]

**– John Francis Mercer, delegate
to Constitutional Convention**

If we want to uphold the Constitution, we have to make _____ _____[44] in choosing our leaders, be part of the process and be engaged in our government.

In our final Episode (7), we will discuss the proper, constitutional way to fulfill our duty in giving or refusing our consent.

Assignments:

In your own words, why is it important to study the *Declaration of Independence* in a class on the *Constitution*?

_____

_____

_____

_____

Using the full text of both documents in Appendix 2 and 3 of this book, compare *Declaration* grievance #3 to Article 1, Section 2, Clause 2 of the *Constitution*. Then find the Clause in the *Constitution* that is connected to the following Grievances in the *Declaration*:

Grievance #4: Article 1, Section 5, Clause ____[45]

Grievance #5: Article 1, Section 4, Clause ____[46]

Grievance #7: Article 1, Section ____[47], Clause 4

Grievance #8: Article ___[48], Section 8, Clause 9

Grievance #11: Article 1, Section ___, Clause ___[49]

Grievance #12: Article ___, Section ___, Clause ___[50]

Grievance #14: The _____[51] Amendment

Grievance #18: The _____ and _____[52] Amendment

The founding fathers believed that a lack of patriotism was selfishness:

> *"Patriotism is as much a virtue as justice, and is as necessary for the support of societies as natural affection is for the support of families.*
>
> *The amor patriae [love of country] is both a moral and a religious duty. It comprehends not only the love of our neighbors but of millions of our fellow creatures, not only of the present but of future generations."*

– Benjamin Rush

EPISODE TWO TAKE AWAYS:

1. The Founders were much like us, from every profession and background; busy with their lives, but willing to give of their lives, fortunes and sacred honor. We can do the same thing.

2. The Founders did not agree on everything. We do not need 100% of Americans to agree on every issue in order to restore our Constitutional Republic. A small percentage of 5% to 7% can move the entire nation in the right direction.

3. We must be patriots, like the Founders, and stand up and defend freedom on our watch.

_____

_____

_____

_____

_____

_____

_____

_____

_____

_____

EPISODE THREE
The Cradle of Liberty

_____ _____[1] is the room where both the Declaration of Independence and the United States Constitution were framed.

_____[2] men debated and contributed to the drafting of the Constitution, but only _____[3] signed the final document.

The Pennsylvania Abolition Society was started by Founding Fathers _____ _____ and _____ _____[4].

On his way to be inaugurated as President of the United States, _____ _____ [5] stopped at Independence Hall and gave an impromptu speech in which he said,

I am filled with deep emotion at finding myself standing here, in this place, where were collected together the wisdom, the patriotism, the devotion to principle, from which sprang the institutions under which we live. You have kindly suggested to me that in my hands is the task of restoring peace to the present distracted condition of the country. I can say in return, Sir, that all the political sentiments I entertain have been drawn, so far as I have been able to draw them, from the sentiments which originated and were given to the world from this hall. I have never had a feeling politically that did not spring from the sentiments embodied in the Declaration of Independence. I have often pondered over the dangers which were incurred by the men who assembled here, and framed and adopted that Declaration of Independence. I have pondered over the toils that were endured by the officers and soldiers of the army who achieved that Independence. I have often inquired of myself what great principle or idea it was that kept this Confederacy so long together. It was not the mere matter of the separation of the Colonies from the motherland; but that sentiment in the Declaration of Independence which gave liberty, not alone to the people of this country, but, I hope, to the world, for all future time. It was that which gave promise that in due time the weight would be lifted from the shoulders of all men. This is the sentiment embodied in that Declaration of Independence. Now, my friends, can this country be saved upon that basis? If it can, I will consider myself one of the happiest men in the world if I can help to save it. If it can't be saved upon that principle, it will be truly awful. But, if this country cannot be saved without giving up that principle--- I was about to say I would rather be assassinated on this spot than to surrender it. Now, in my view of the present aspect of affairs, there is no need of bloodshed and war. There is no necessity for it. I am not in favor of such a course, and I may say in advance, there will be no blood shed unless it be forced upon the Government. The Government will not use force unless force is used against it. My friends, this is a wholly unprepared speech. I did not expect to be called upon to say a word when I came here---I supposed I was merely to do something towards raising a flag. I may, therefore, have said something indiscreet, but I have said nothing but what I am willing to live by, and, in the pleasure of Almighty God, die by.

Four years later, 85,000 mourners would pay tribute and pass by his body lying in state at Independence Hall for two days.

_____[6] Hall is the room where George Washington was inaugurated as President in and John Adams was inaugurated as President in 1796.

The Bill of Rights was proposed by Congress on _____[7] while they were meeting in _____ _____[8].

On December 15, 1791, while meeting in _____[9], Congress was informed by President _____[10] that enough states had ratified the Bill of Rights.

How many Amendments were originally proposed in the Bill of Rights? _____[11]

How many Amendments were ultimately ratified? _____[12] in 1791 and _____[13] in 1992.

The following message is on the _____ _____ [14]:

"Proclaim Liberty Throughout All the Land Unto All the Inhabitants thereof"

The _____ [15] House (or sometimes called The Declaration House) is where _____ _____ [16] worked on drafting the Declaration of Independence.

"We the people of the United States, in order to form a more perfect Union, establish justice, insure domestic tranquility, provide for the common defense, promote the general welfare, and secure the blessings of liberty to ourselves and our posterity, do ordain and establish this Constitution for the United States of America."

– Preamble to the Constitution

The most powerful branch of government is the _____ [17] branch, because we have a chance to replace them every _____ [18] years.

The founders stated that the _____[19] branch was the weakest of the three "by far."

****

General Welfare: *"Exemption from any unusual evil or calamity; the enjoyment of peace and prosperity, or the ordinary blessings of society and civil government; applied to states."* (emphasis added)

– Webster's 1828 Dictionary

"General welfare" is not "_____ _____[20]," it only applies to the states and the system in general.

Original Intent of "General Welfare" is very different from today's meaning of the phrase. Unless the Constitution is amended, which meaning should we use for constitutional interpretation? Today's understanding or Original Intent (that of the time the phrase was placed in the Constitution)? _____   _____[21]

_____

_____

_____

_____

_____

_____

_____

_____

_____

_____

_____

_____

_____

_____

_____

_____

_____

_____

_____

U.S. CONSTITUTION AT A GLANCE

ARTICLES

I	=	_____ [22]
II	=	_____ [23]
III	=	_____ [24]
IV	=	_____ [25]
V	=	_____ [26]
VI	=	_____ [27]
VII	=	_____ [28]

AMENDMENTS

1-10	=	_____ [29]
12*, 20, 22, 23, 25	=	_____ [30]
11	=	_____ [31]
17, 20, 27	=	_____ [32]
13, 14, 15	=	_____ [33]
15, 19, 24, 26	=	_____ [34]
16	=	_____ [35]
18, 21	=	_____ [36]

BILL OF RIGHTS

1st	=	_____ [37]
2nd	=	_____ [38]
3rd	=	_____ [39]
4th	=	_____ [40]
5th	=	_____ [41]
6th	=	_____ [42]
7th	=	_____ [43]
8th	=	_____ [44]
9th	=	_____ [45]
10th	=	_____ [46]

NOTE: Several copies of the filled in *Constitution At a Glance* are in Appendix A

*12th Amendment Note regarding video comments: The 1800 rematch election between Adams and Jefferson also created confusion when the old process created a tie in the electoral college between Jefferson and his running mate Aaron Burr due to there being no distinction between electoral votes cast for President or Vice-President. The tie threw the election to Congress, which finally chose Jefferson after several dozen ballots.

The _____ [47] Amendment limited any person to serve as president to no more than two full terms, thereby curbing the power of the executive branch. This was ratified after _____ _____ _____ [48] was elected to a fourth presidential term and the American people had decided that was too long and too much power.

The District of Columbia was designed by Article 1, Section 8, Paragraph 17 not to be a _____ [49] or within a _____ [50], but rather a special place for the seat of the federal government.

The 23rd Amendment gives citizens in D.C. the right to _____ for _____ [51] by granting D.C. the same number of electors in the electoral college as the smallest state.

The _____[52] Amendment changed the way _____[53] are elected, removing the check and balance of states' ability to curb federal encroachment upon state jurisdictions.

The 27th Amendment was originally the _____[54] Amendment in the Bill of Rights adopted by Congress in 1789 and proposed to the states for ratification.

_____ _____[55] resurrected and ultimately pushed through ratification of the 27th Amendment.

The 14th Amendment _____[56] the Constitution to the states, not just the Federal government.

For a detailed description of the history of the 14th Amendment, read Justice Clarence Thomas' Concurring Opinion in McDonald v. Chicago and his argument for why the 14th guarantees all citizens the same privileges and immunities. You can view the opinion online here:

http://www.law.cornell.edu/supct/html/08-1521.ZC1.html

The "voting" amendments were significant because the majority was giving the _____[57] the ability to _____[58], which is rarely seen in other countries.

The _____[59] Amendment was necessary for Congress to ban alcohol because the people had never given them, through the Constitution, the authority to do so.

Before the 17th Amendment, the House protected the interests of the _____[60], and the Senate protected the interests of the _____[61].

After the 17th Amendment, Congress became like a giant _____ _____ _____[62].

The Constitution defines what the Federal government can do, and the Bill of Rights defines what they cannot do.

"The power under the Constitution will always be in the people. It is entrusted for certain defined purposes, and for a certain limited period to representatives of their own choosing;

and whenever it is exercised contrary to their interest or not agreeably to their wishes, their servants can and undoubtedly will be recalled."

– George Washington

EPISODE THREE TAKE AWAYS:

1. Repealing the 17th Amendment would restore the Senate and protections of liberty.

2. The only proper way to amend the Constitution is through Article V involving the states (and NOT through the courts).

_____

_____

_____

_____

_____

_____

_____

_____

_____

EPISODE FOUR
Congressional Do's and Don'ts

A _____ _____[1] is one that recognizes jurisdictional lines – to understand what belongs to government and what does not, not one that is necessarily small in size.

The founding fathers said that the "general welfare" clause was not to be interpreted as saying an industry was too big to fail and needs a bailout, during the debates concerning bailing out the codfish industry in 1791.

"If Congress can employ money indefinitely to the general welfare, and are the sole and supreme judges of the general welfare, they may take the care of religion into their own hands; they may appoint teachers in every State, county and parish and pay them out of their public treasury; they may take into their own hands the education of children, establishing in like manner schools throughout the Union; they may assume the provision of the poor; they may undertake the regulation of all roads other than post-roads; in short, everything, from the highest object of state legislation down to the most minute object of police, would be thrown under the power of Congress. ... Were the power of Congress to be established in the latitude contended for, it would subvert the very foundations, and transmute the very nature of the limited Government established by the people of America."

– James Madison

****

What is the one Constitutional question census workers should ask at each home? _____

2

- **Section 8 of the Constitution contains DO's for the** _____ _____ [3]

- **Section 9 of the Constitution contains DON'Ts for the** _____ _____ [4]

- **Section 10 of the Constitution contains DON'Ts for the** _____ [5]

Congress cannot add power ____ _____[6]; it only comes from us.

Congress has the power to collect taxes for these purposes:

- To pay the _____[7]
- To provide for the common _____[8] and general _____[9] of the United State

The founders believed that to carry debt over to the next generation is _____[10].

Hamilton said that the test for spending money Constitutionally is whether it is for a _____[11] purpose or a _____[12] purpose.

"Consider for a moment the immeasurable difference between the Constitution limited in its powers to the enumerated objects, and expounded as it would be by the import claimed for the phraseology in question.

"The difference is equivalent to two Constitutions, of characters essentially contrasted with each other--the one possessing powers confined to certain specified cases, the other extended to all cases whatsoever;...

"Can less be said...than that it is impossible that such a Constitution as the latter would have been recommended to the States by all the members of that body whose names were subscribed to the instrument? ... Is it credible that such a power would have been unnoticed and unopposed in the Federal Convention? In the State Conventions, which contended for, and and proposed restrictive and explanatory amendments? And in the Congress of 1789, which recommended so many of these amendments? A power to impose unlimited taxes for unlimited purposes could never have escaped...those public bodies.

"Constitution is a limited one, possessing no power not actually given, and carrying on the face of it a distrust of power beyond the distrust indicated by the ordinary forms of free Government."[xxvi]

– James Madison

A balanced budget amendment to the Constitution failed in 1999 by how many votes? _____ [13]

"Regulate commerce" means "make _____ [14]," not "micromanage."

Congress has the power to regulate commerce:

- with _____ [15] nations
- Between the several _____ [16]
- With the _____ _____ [17]

This was not a license to _____-_____ [18] the market.

Jefferson said that "The pillars of our prosperity are the most thriving when left most free to _____ _____ [19]."

The founders were specific about everything in the Constitution because they had a real _____ of _____ [20].

Our system has separation of powers between the _____ of _____ [21] as well as the branches.

"Nothing is more certain, than that the forms of liberty may be retained, when the substance is gone. In government, as well as in religion, 'The letter killeth, but the spirit giveth life.'"
– John Dickinson, Constitution Signer

It is important to follow the _____ [22] of the "general welfare" clause and the rest of the Constitution, rather than trying to squeeze a new meaning out of the wording.

_____

_____

_____

_____

The founding father responsible for the "promote the progress of science & useful arts" clause was Noah Webster.

The only Constitutional way to *"promote the progress of science and useful arts"* is through _____, _____, _____[23], and other intellectual property protections; NOT through subsidies.

When you spend your money buying something for yourself, _____[24] matters and _____[25] matters.

When you spend your money to buy someone else something, _____[26] doesn't matter quite as much, but _____[27] still does.

When you spend someone else's money to buy another person something, neither _____ or _____[28] matter much.

Every government transaction is a third-party transaction, so _____ and _____[29] never matter.

Limited   Government   means   _____
_____[30].

Even if it's an incredible work of art, it is not
_____ _____[31] to fund it.

Case in point: with _____ _____
_____[32] research, government is funding science that
doesn't work, because politics has entered into the
equation.

The Constitution gives Congress the power to
_____ _____[33], but does not specify how that
declaration is to be made.

The first war against radical Islamist terrorism
began in _____[34].

The "Letters of marque" provision referred to
_____[35] hired to help rescue our sailors from
the Barbary pirates.

Congress has the power to make all laws which shall be necessary and proper for carrying into execution the _____[36] powers.

"Shall we establish nothing good because we know it cannot be eternal? Shall we live without government because every constitution has its old age and its period? Because we know that we shall die, shall we take no pains to preserve or lengthen our life?...

"Far from it, Sir: it only requires the more watchful attention to settle government upon the best principles and in the wisest manner that it may last as long as the nature of things will permit."

– John Witherspoon

"All that the best men can do is to persevere in doing their duty to their country and leave the consequences to Him Who made it their duty, being neither elated by success, however great, nor discouraged by disappointment, however frequent and mortifying."

"We must go home to be happy, and our home is not in this world. Here we have nothing to do but our duty, and by it to regulate our business and our pleasure."

– John Jay, first Supreme Court Chief Justice

EPISODE FOUR TAKE AWAYS:

1. Remember Jurisdictions!

2. Verify the meaning of words in the Constitution based on their definition at the time, not by what they mean today.

_____

_____

_____

_____

_____

_____

_____

_____

_____

_____

_____

_____

EPISODE FIVE
Of Kings and Courts

"The interest of the people is one thing: it is the public interest. And where the public interest governs, it is a government of laws and not of men.

"The interest of a king or of a party is another thing: it is a private interest. And where private interest governs, it is a nation of men and not of laws." — **John Adams**

The _____[1], more than any other entity, is the one who decides whether we are a government of laws or a government of men.

The Electoral College is a way for the _____ [2] to have a voice, and the _____ [3] to have a voice in the election of the President.

The Founders rejected having the President elected by _____ _____ [4] because the most populated areas would outvote the more rural areas.

The Founding Fathers used the Electoral College to strike a balance that would require the winner to have both a _____ _____ [5] of the people AND a sufficient _____ [6] of the vote.

In a popular vote scenario, the major deciders for the Presidency would be the _____ _____ [7].

"I view great cities as pestilential to the morals, the health, and the liberties of man."

– Thomas Jefferson, writing to Benjamin Rush

"I agree with you in your opinion of cities. Cowper the poet very happily expresses our ideas of them compared with the country. 'God made the country; man made cities.' I consider them in the same light that I do abscesses on the human body – as reservoirs of all the impurities of a community."

– Benjamin Rush, writing back to Jefferson

Supporters of National Popular Vote want _____ _____[8], rather than a constitutional republic.

"Pure democracy cannot subsist long nor be carried far into the departments of state – it is very subject to caprice and the madness of popular rage."

– John Witherspoon, Signer of the Declaration of Independence

"Remember, democracy never lasts long. It soon wastes, exhausts, and murders itself. There never was a democracy yet that did not commit suicide."[xxvii]

– John Adams

"A simple democracy is one of the greatest of evils. A democracy is a mobocracy."[xxviii]

– Benjamin Rush, Signer of the Declaration

Section _____[9] of the 25th Amendment is the process by which the President declares he/she is unable to fulfill the duties of the presidency.

Section _____[10] of the 25th Amendment is the process by which the VP and a majority of the Cabinet declare the President unable to fulfill the duties of the presidency.

When has the 25th Amendment been invoked under Section 4? _____[11].

At the time of this recording, the only time the 25th Amendment was invoked under Section 3 was once by President _____[12] and twice by President _____[13].

The Constitution requires Congress to assemble ___ _____ _____[14] in every year.

During the days of the Founding Fathers, recesses could last for _____[15].

Recess appointments were designed to deal with an _____ _____[16] that occurs during a recess, not to sneak through an appointment that the Senate had refused to approve while it was in Session.

The President has the power to make appointments or even create "czars" within an agency that Congress created by _____[17].

Article 1, Section 5, requires approval from the other chamber for either the House or Senate to _____[18] for more than three days during the Session.

The practice of issuing Executive Orders started with President _____[19].

Executive Orders are Constitutional as long as they are executing a law that _____[20] has actually _____[21].

Most of Calvin Coolidge's 1,203 Executive Orders were made to repeal Woodrow Wilson's 1,803 Executive Orders.

"If the president alone was vested with the power of appointing all officers, and was left to select a council for himself, he would be liable to be deceived by flatterers and pretenders to patriotism, who would have no motive but their own emolument [self-seeking profit and gain]."

– Roger Sherman, Declaration of Independence and Constitution Signer

****

_____

_____

_____

_____

_____

_____

_____

_____

Four Myths of the Judiciary

Samuel Adams complained about judicial tyranny in the form of _____ ___ _____[22] and _____ _____[23] as far back as 1765.

Myth #1: The three branches are co-equal.

The Federalist Papers were written by _____, _____, and _____[24] and are like an instruction manual for the Constitution.

In Federalist Paper 51, Madison said the _____[25] branch "necessarily predominates" because it is the branch that is _____ to the _____[26].

In Federalist Paper 78, Hamilton said the _____[27] was the weakest branch and would not be a threat to our liberty if it remained in its proper jurisdiction.

"...the judiciary is beyond comparison the weakest of the three departments of power; ...the general liberty of the people can never be endangered from that quarter; I mean so long as the judiciary remains truly distinct from both the legislature and the Executive... And it proves, in the last place, that as liberty can have nothing to fear from the judiciary alone, but would have every thing to fear from its union with either of the other departments; The judiciary... has no influence over either the sword or the purse; no direction either of the strength or of the wealth of the society; and can take no active resolution whatever. It may truly be said to have neither force nor will, but merely judgment; and must ultimately depend upon the aid of the executive arm even for the efficacy of its judgments."

– Alexander Hamilton, Federalist 78

The judiciary was established by and is accountable to the other _____ _____[28] of government, because they owe a _____[29] to the people.

The Constitution leaves it entirely to the discretion of _____[30] as to how many members will be on the court and how many lower courts to establish from time to time.

Congress may also set the _____[31], removing issues from the purview of the court.

> *"The provision of the act of 1867, affirming the appellate jurisdiction of this court in cases of habeas corpus is expressly repealed. It is hardly possible to imagine a plainer instance of positive exception. We are not at liberty to inquire into the motives of the legislature. We can only examine into its power under the Constitution; and the power to make exceptions to the appellate jurisdiction of this court is given by express words. Without jurisdiction the court cannot proceed at all in any cause... It is quite clear, therefore, that this court cannot proceed to pronounce judgment in this case, for it has no longer jurisdiction of the appeal; and judicial duty is not less fitly performed by declining ungranted jurisdiction than in exercising firmly that which the Constitution and the laws confer."*

– U.S. Supreme Court in *Ex Parte McCardle*[xxix]

Myth #2: Federal judges hold lifetime appointments.

Judges are *not* appointed for life, they are appointed for _____ _____[32].

The House of Representatives has the power to impeach *(essentially an indictment, not a finding of guilt or innocence)* and the Senate has the sole power to _____[33] all impeachments.

Judges have been impeached for:

- Issuing an order _____[34] an act of Congress
- Drunkenness in private life
- _____[35] in the courtroom
- Profanity
- Judicial _____-_____[36]

According to Hamilton, impeachment is a _____[37] in the hands of the legislature.

Myth #3: The primary responsibility of the judiciary is to protect the minority from the majority.

The fundamental principle of our Constitution requires that the will of the _____[38] shall prevail.

"The fundamental principle of our Constitution enjoins [requires] that the will of the majority shall prevail."
– George Washington

Every person should have _____[39] protection under the law.

Myth #4: Only judges are capable of determining Constitutionality and their primary responsibility is judicial review.

_____ _____[40] has a say in determining Constitutionality of a law or action.

"It is quite foreign from the nature of the judiciary's office to make them judges of the policy of public measures."
– Elbridge Gerry

[T]he opinion which gives to the judges the right to decide what laws are constitutional and what not, not only for themselves, in their own sphere of action, but for the Legislature and Executive also in their spheres, would make the Judiciary a despotic branch.[xxx]
– Thomas Jefferson

The Constitution, on this hypothesis, is a mere thing of wax in the hands of the judiciary, which they may twist, and shape into any form they please.[xxxi]

– Thomas Jefferson

Nothing has yet been offered to invalidate the doctrine that the meaning of the Constitution may as well be ascertained by the Legislative as by the Judicial authority.[xxxii]

– James Madison

The _____[41] is the place to decide the policy of public measures, not the courts.

"Members of this court are vested with the authority to interpret the law; we possess neither the expertise nor the prerogative to make policy judgments. Those decisions are entrusted to our Nation's elected leaders, who can be thrown out of office if the people disagree with them. It is not our job to protect the people from the consequences of their political choices."

– Supreme Court Chief Justice John Roberts in *NFIB v. Sebelius*

EPISODE FIVE TAKE AWAYS:

1. Hold every president accountable to their limited powers and do not support any president making law by themselves, even if it is a law you want to see happen.

2. The Courts should NOT be making law from the bench. We must get rid of the COURTstitution and get back to the design of our constitutional republic.

3. Support Patriot Academy to prepare the next generation!   PatriotAcademy.com

_____

_____

_____

_____

_____

_____

_____

_____

EPISODE SIX
The Bill of Rights

The purpose of government is to secure inalienable rights, which is the function of the Bill of Rights.

Signer of the Declaration John Dickinson defined an inalienable right as a right *"which God gave to you and no inferior power has a right to take away."*

"[Human governments] could not give the rights essential to happiness... We claim them from a higher source – from the King of kings and Lord of all the earth. They are not annexed to us by parchments and seals. They are created in us by the decrees of Providence, which establish the laws of our nature. They are born with us; exist with us; and cannot be taken from us by any human power, without taking our lives."

– John Dickinson, Constitution Signer

The five fundamental freedoms in the **First Amendment** are _____, _____, _____, _____, and _____ [1].

John Quincy Adams believed so strongly in the right to petition one's government that he would present petitions in Congress even when he disagreed with them.

James Madison called conscience *"the most sacred of property."*

"For what business, in the name of common sense, has the magistrate with our religion? The state does not have any concern in the matter. In what manner does it affect society in what outward form we think it best to pay our adoration to God? The consciences of men are not the objects of human legislation. In contrast with this spiritual tyranny, how beautiful appears our constitution in disclaiming all jurisdiction over the souls of men, securing by a never-to-be-repealed section the voluntary, unchecked moral persuasion of every person by his own self-directed communication with the Father of spirits!"

– William Livingston, Constitution Signer

"Security under our constitution is given to the rights of conscience and private judgment. They are by nature subject to no control but that of Deity, and in that free situation they are now left."

– John Jay, first Supreme Court Chief Justice

Starting in 1640, the top issue that brought people to America was the rights of conscience.

"Congress shall make no law respecting an establishment of religion, or prohibiting the free exercise thereof. . . ." [xxxiii]

Where in the Constitution is the phrase *"separation of church and state?"* _____ [2]

To understand the "intent" of the legislators who pass any law, one must look at the _____ [3] where the discussions that took place at the time the law was being debated were recorded.

Article ____, Section ____[4] of the *Constitution* requires that everything said on the floor of the House and Senate be recorded in a journal.[xxxiv]

How many times do the Annals of Congress record the phrase *"separation of church and state"* during the debates drafting the First Amendment? _____[5]

The phrase appears in a letter from _____ _____[6] to the Danbury Baptists, assuring them that government would not _____[7] on their freedom of religion.

James Madison said that the intent of the First Amendment was to prevent a _____ _____ _____[8], like the Church of England.

Two days after writing the phrase *"separation of church and state,"* Thomas Jefferson attended the weekly church service held at _____[9].[xxxv]

The most active and influential man of the Constitutional Convention and author of the Preamble was _____ _____[10].

"Religion is the only solid basis of good morals. Therefore, education should teach the precepts of religion and the duties of man toward God."[xxxvi]

– Gouverneur Morris, Signer of the Constitution

_____ _____[11] signed the Declaration, the Constitution, and served on the original Supreme Court.

"Human law must rest its authority ultimately upon the authority of that law which is divine.   Far from being rivals or enemies, religion and law are twin sisters, friends, and mutual assistants. Indeed, these two sciences run into each other."[xxxvii]

– James Wilson,

Signer of the Constitution

THE SECOND AMENDMENT IS COVERED IN DEPTH IN EPISODE ONE (see pages 11 through 15)

The **3rd Amendment** prohibits the _____ ___ _____[12] in homes during peacetime without the owner's permission, and requires it to be done in a manner _____ ____ _____[13] during wartime.

The **4th Amendment** protects us from unreasonable _____ and _____[14].

The only exception in the **5th Amendment** to the right to a Grand Jury indictment for capital offenses is for the _____[15] during wartime.

Many _____[16] violate the **5th Amendment** today by devaluing private property without _____[17].

The **6th Amendment** guarantees, among other things, our right to a _____ _____ jury

_____[18], to confront our accusers (witnesses), and to have an _____[19].

The **7th Amendment** guarantees the right to a jury trial in civil cases when the amount in controversy is at least _____[20].

In _____ _____[21], the jury can determine not only the violation of the law, but the justice of the law itself and its application.

The **8th Amendment** prevents excessive _____[22] or _____[23], as well as _____ & _____[24] punishments.

The **10th Amendment** reiterates that the powers of the government are limited (bucket with a lid on it) to the specifics in the Constitution, while the 9th Amendment says the opposite for the people, namely that our personal rights are not limited by those _____[25] in the Constitution.

Any additional rights read into the Constitution must not violate _____ _____[26] of the Constitution or the _____[27].

George Mason did not sign the Constitution because it did not _____ _____[28], and because he wanted more _____[29] placed around government.

"Government is instituted to protect property. This being the end of government, that alone is a just government which impartially secures to every man whatever is his own. It is not a just government, nor is property secure under it, where arbitrary restrictions deny to part of its citizens that free use of their faculties or where the property which a man has in his personal safety and personal liberty is violated by arbitrary seizures of one class of citizens for the service of the rest."

– James Madison

EPISODE SIX TAKE AWAYS:

1. The purpose of the Bill of Rights was to remind all of us that these rights do not come from government, they are from the laws of nature and Government's job is to protect them.

2. The 2nd Amendment is the palladium of all our other freedoms.

3. We must teach the next generation how to use firearms and defend themselves and teach them the Constitution and how to be good citizens.

4. Bring your family to Front Sight!

_____

_____

_____

_____

_____

_____

_____

EPISODE SEVEN
The Duty of Citizens

Article ____[1] gives two options for how to amend the Constitution.

Option 1: Congressional Proposals

When _____[2] of both the House and Senate adopt proposed Amendments, they are sent to the states for ratification and _____[3] of the states must ratify for the Amendment to become part of the Constitution.

Option 2: State Proposals

When _____[4] of the states apply, the Congress must call a convention of the states for proposing amendments. Any amendments proposed at the convention must still be ratified by _____[5] of the states before the Amendment would become part of the Constitution.

Possible Amendments

- **Balanced Budget Amendment**

- **Parental Rights Amendment -** The U.N. Treaty on the Rights of the Child, if adopted, would be equal to the _____[6] and above _____ _____[7]. Also, many state CPS organizations are overstepping their bounds. (www.ParentalRights.org)

- **Term Limits** – It is bad for both the _____[8] and for the _____[9] themselves to have long-term careers in the legislature. In addition, term limits tend to keep legislators focused on getting the job done.

- **Define Term of Federal Judges**

****

All it takes to kill a Constitutional amendment is one legislative body from each of only 13 states.

It does not endanger the Constitution to use the Constitution.

A convention of states is a way for the states to push back against encroachment from the Federal government.

The states can recall their delegates to the Convention of States if the delegates do not honor the wishes of their respective states.

Visit www.ConventionOfStates.com for more information.

****

<u>Three things NOT to do</u>

_____ 10

_____ 11

_____ 12

The historical case for nullification is based on the Virginia and Kentucky resolutions passed against the _____ and _____[13] acts during Adams' presidency.

Three reasons the others states rejected the Virginia and Kentucky resolutions:

1. _____ _____[14] for determining the constitutionality of laws is at the federal level, not the state legislatures.

2. It _____[15] the federal election process.

3. It is "…of a _____ tendency…" because it creates _____[16].

"But it follows, from no view of the subject, that a nullification of a law of the U. S. can as is now contended, belong rightfully to a single State, as one of the parties to the Constitution; the State not ceasing to avow its adherence to the Constitution. A plainer contradiction in terms, or a more fatal inlet to anarchy, cannot be imagined."

– James Madison in response to the South Carolina nullification crisis of the early 1830s

Nullification would place _____[17] power over _____[18] power.

When Congress passes a bad law, we have two constitutional options:

1. Convince the majority of the nation to _____ _____[19].

2. Convince the _____[20] to rule the law _____[21].

_____[22] reminded Americans that changes must be made only by using *"...the way which the Constitution designates. But let there be no change by usurpation; for though this in one instance may be the instrument of good, it is the customary weapon by which free governments are destroyed."*[xxxviii]

For more information on nullification, See Appendix D: *Limiting an Overreaching Federal Government: Is State Nullification the Solution? A Constitutional Analysis by David Barton.*

What TO do

To influence ARTICLES 1 & 2:

_____!23 The first place in the Constitution a citizen is given responsibility is the word _____24 in Article 1, Section 2.

Rick lost his first race by only ____25 votes out of over 30,000, then won on the recount by _____26 votes.

The 2000 Presidential election was determined by a mere _____27 votes in Florida.

> *"Let it be impressed on your mind that God commands you to choose for rulers just men who will rule in the fear of God.... [I]f the citizens neglect their duty and place unprincipled men in office, the government will soon be corrupted ... If [our] government fails to secure public prosperity and happiness, it must be because the citizens neglect the Divine commands, and elect bad men to make and administer the laws."xxxix*
>
> **– Noah Webster**

The right to choose our _____[28] is something most people in the history of the world never got to do!

The three ingredients in the "mixing bowl" of the American system:

1. Knowledge of the people – before we can choose wisely at the polls, we must know the _____[29] by which to measure the candidates.

2. The pool of _____[30] – find good people with leadership skills and ask them to run!

3. The _____[31] of the citizens – impact the political process by knocking on doors, making phone calls, contributing, etc.

A _____[32] is only thinking about the next election. A _____[33] is concerned about the next generation!

To influence ARTICLE 3:

- Influence who the _____[34] are who approve justices

- Get involved with the _____[35] judiciary

- _____[36] legal organizations like the Alliance Defending Freedom, ACLJ, Pacific Justice Institution, Liberty Counsel, etc.

To influence ARTICLE 4:

Educate people on how we are a _____[37], not a democracy.

More ideas:

- Adopt a potential _____[38] to the Constitution as your project

- Watch out for treaties: keep up with them and call your Senators when necessary

- Live out the Bill of Rights!

"Finally ye . . . whose power it is to save or destroy your country, consider well the important trust . . . which God... has put into your hands. To God and posterity, you are accountable for them. . . Let not your children have reason to curse you for giving up those rights, and prostrating those institutions which your fathers delivered to you."[xl]

– Reverend Matthias Burnett

"DUTY IS OURS, RESULTS ARE GOD'S."
– John Quincy Adams

****

EPISODE SEVEN TAKE AWAYS:

1. Read Mark Levin's Liberty Amendments and research ConventionOfStates.com to put the federal government back inside proper jurisdictions.

2. Have a generational view and do your duty whether you see the results or not.

3. Look for the positives, the victories; and share the good news with others. Listen to Good News Friday on WallBuildersLive.com.

4. Become students of freedom. Go back through this course multiple times and seek out other sources of education.

_____

_____

_____

_____

_____

_____

APPENDIX A:
CONSTITUTION AT A GLANCE

Enclosed are several copies of the *Constitution At A Glance* for you to tear out and use in class, or put in your purse/wallet, or stick on the mirror to memorize, or share with a friend.

U.S. CONSTITUTION AT A GLANCE

ARTICLES:

I	=	Congress
II	=	Presidency
III	=	Courts
IV	=	States; Republic
V	=	Amendment Process
VI	=	Debts, Supremacy, oath, no religious test
VII	=	Ratification & Attestation

AMENDMENTS:

1 -10	=	Bill of Rights (see below)
12, 20, 22, 23, 25	=	Presidency
11	=	Judiciary (suits against states)
17, 20, 27	=	Congress (Sen elections, terms, $$$)
13, 14, 15	=	End slavery & establish Civil Rights
15, 19, 24, 26	=	Voting Rights (race, gender, $$$, age)
16	=	Income Tax
18 & 21	=	To drink or not to drink

BILL OF RIGHTS:

1st	=	religion; speech; press; assembly; petition
2nd	=	individual right to bear arms
3rd	=	quartering of soldiers
4th	=	searches & seizures
5th	=	Grand Jury; Double Jeopardy; Self-Incrimination; Due Process; private property takings clause
6th	=	speedy public jury trial; witnesses; attorney
7th	=	civil jury trial
8th	=	excessive fines & bail; cruel & unusual
9th	=	individual rights not enumerated or limited
10th	=	fed rights limited/enumerated; rest left to states/people

U.S. CONSTITUTION AT A GLANCE

ARTICLES:

I	=	Congress
II	=	Presidency
III	=	Courts
IV	=	States; Republic
V	=	Amendment Process
VI	=	Debts, Supremacy, oath, no religious test
VII	=	Ratification & Attestation

AMENDMENTS:

1 -10	=	Bill of Rights (see below)
12, 20, 22, 23, 25	=	Presidency
11	=	Judiciary (suits against states)
17, 20, 27	=	Congress (Sen elections, terms, $$$)
13, 14, 15	=	End slavery & establish Civil Rights
15, 19, 24, 26	=	Voting Rights (race, gender, $$$, age)
16	=	Income Tax
18 & 21	=	To drink or not to drink

BILL OF RIGHTS:

1st	=	religion; speech; press; assembly; petition
2nd	=	individual right to bear arms
3rd	=	quartering of soldiers
4th	=	searches & seizures
5th	=	Grand Jury; Double Jeopardy; Self-Incrimination; Due Process; private property takings clause
6th	=	speedy public jury trial; witnesses; attorney
7th	=	civil jury trial
8th	=	excessive fines & bail; cruel & unusual
9th	=	individual rights not enumerated or limited
10th	=	fed rights limited/enumerated; rest left to states/people

Appendix B:

**Limiting an Overreaching Federal Government:
Is State Nullification the Solution?
A Constitutional Analysis**

By David Barton

Appendix B:
Limiting an Overreaching Federal Government:
Is State Nullification the Solution?
A Constitutional Analysis By David Barton

Periodically, important words and concepts are invoked that are relatively unknown today but which nevertheless have a lengthy historical and constitutional background (e.g. "attainder," the "Exceptions Clause," the "Sundays Excepted Clause," the "Supremacy Clause," etc.). The danger is that when important terms become unfamiliar to citizens, they can be severed from their original meanings and given new interpretations that not only are unwarranted by the Constitution but even negate its intent.

For example, in 1998, Bill Clinton was accused of committing perjury and obstruction of justice while president, [1] but his supporters argued that these crimes did not rise to the level of impeachable offenses because they were not "high crimes" under the Constitution.[2] (They argued that "high crimes" did not include felonies in a civil proceeding but rather criminal felonies such as treason, murder, etc.)[3]. Yet the historic definition of "high crimes" in the Constitution was a wrongdoing committed by a person in a "high" office (such as the president or a federal judge, in contrast to a local school board member or city dogcatcher). Therefore, a civil felony committed in office by the president did indeed constitute a "high crime" and definitely was an impeachable offense, but few citizens understood this because they were unfamiliar with that clause of the Constitution.

Another similarly misunderstood but recently resurrected historic term is "nullification." The revived use of this term has been the result of widespread dissatisfaction with federal intrusion into many areas that were formerly the sole domain of the states (e.g., education, transportation, health care, energy policy, etc.). Some leaders are now advocating state nullification as a constitutional solution – that a state has the right to declare a federal law unconstitutional, thereby nullifying that law.

For example, Texas gubernatorial candidate Debra Medina asserts:

> *Texas must stop the overreaching federal government and nullify federal mandates in agriculture, energy, education, healthcare, industry, and any other areas D. C. is not granted authority by Article I, Section 8 of the U. S. Constitution....It is our duty as a state to recognize when Washington D. C. is stepping outside its constitutional bounds. Jefferson further commented that nullification by the states of all unauthorized acts is the rightful remedy....We must use the tools of nullification and interposition aggressively.* [4]

And U. S. Congressman and presidential candidate Ron Paul also supports nullification:

> *I think it's a great idea....[I] think it's going to grow in importance. And I think it's going to grow because the government, the federal government will be seen as inept and ineffective. And I think it'll almost be de facto in the sense that the states will eventually just ignore some of the mandates.* [5]

Did the Founding Fathers – the Framers of our government – give states the constitutional power to nullify federal laws? As will be seen in the historical evidence presented below, the answer is an unequivocal "No!"; they did not give that power to states. In fact, every major Founder condemned this type of state nullification – including Thomas Jefferson, who is wrongly invoked above as approving it.

Notwithstanding this fact, there is little doubt that they took definite steps to ensure that the federal government would not intrude into state issues through the Tenth Amendment to the Constitution:

The powers not delegated to the United States by the Constitution, nor prohibited by it to the States, are reserved to the States respectively, or to the people.

Under the Tenth Amendment, everything not specifically enumerated in the Constitution was to remain the purview of the states. As explained by Thomas Jefferson (on numerous occasions):

I consider the foundation of the Constitution as laid on this ground: that "all powers not delegated to the United States by the Constitution, nor prohibited by it to the states, are reserved to the states or to the people."...To take a single step beyond the boundaries thus specially drawn around the powers of Congress is to take possession of a boundless field of power, no longer susceptible of any definition. [6]

The capital and leading object of the Constitution was to leave with the states all authorities which respected their own citizens only, and to transfer to the United States those which respected citizens of foreign or other states....Can any good be effected by taking from the states the moral rule of their citizens and subordinating it to the general [federal] authority?...Such an intention was impossible and...[would] break up the foundations of the Union.... I believe the states can best govern our home concerns, and the general [federal] government our foreign ones. I wish, therefore...never to see all offices transferred to Washington, where, further withdrawn from the eyes of the people, they may more secretly be bought and sold as at market. [7]

Our country is too large to have all its affairs directed by a single [federal] government. Public servants at such a distance, and from under the eye of their constituents, must, from the circumstance of distance, be unable to administer and overlook all the details necessary for the good government of the citizens and...will invite the public agents to corruption, plunder, and waste. [8]

James Madison agreed. In fact, in 1792 when a proposal was made for the federal government to bailout a failing industry and prop it up with federal subsidies, Madison condemned that measure, first noting:

[T]hose who proposed the Constitution conceived [i.e., believed]... (and those who ratified the Constitution conceived) that this is not an indefinite [unrestricted] government...but a limited government tied down to the specified powers....It was never...supposed or suspected that the old Congress could give away the money of the states to bounties to encourage agriculture, or for any other purpose they pleased. [9]

Madison then warned that if the federal government was not kept limited, it would soon usurp state jurisdictions:

If Congress can employ money indefinitely to the "general welfare," and are the sole and supreme judges of the "general welfare," [then Congress might] take the care of religion into their own hands; they may appoint teachers in every state, county, and parish and pay them out of their public treasury; they may take into their own hands the education of children, establishing in like manner schools throughout the Union; they may assume the provision for the poor; they may undertake the regulation of all roads other than [the] post-roads; in short, everything from the highest object of state legislation down to the most minute object of police would be thrown under the power of [the federal] Congress. [10]

Justice Joseph Story (a "Father of American Jurisprudence") affirmed the same constitutional design in his classic 1833 *Commentaries on the Constitution of the United States* (a three-volume work still used by Congress and courts today). Of the Tenth Amendment, Story explained:

Being an instrument of limited and enumerated powers, it follows irresistibly that what is not conferred is withheld and belongs to the state authorities....All powers not delegated...and not prohibited are reserved [to the states]. [11]

Others Founders affirmed the same intent, including Samuel Adams, [12] Patrick Henry, [13] George Mason, [14] James Wilson, [15] Elbridge Gerry, [16] Thomas McKean, [17] Richard Henry Lee, [18] Luther Martin, [19] James Monroe, [20] and many others.

Given the Framers' clear vision of a small and limited federal government, how did it become so large and all-encompassing? The first reason had been foreseen by Founding Father Samuel Adams ("The Father of the American Revolution"), who cautioned:

If the liberties of America are ever completely ruined...it will in all probability be the consequence of a mistaken notion of prudence which leads men to acquiesce in measures of the most destructive tendency for the sake of present ease. [21]

The first step in losing control of the federal government was that it became easier and more convenient to "acquiesce" (i.e., give in) and let the federal government begin doing things never before permitted. The federal government then felt emboldened to enter additional areas – or to use a description provided by Thomas Jefferson, it began *"working like gravity by night and by day, gaining a little today and a little tomorrow, and advancing its noiseless step like a thief, over the field of jurisdiction, until all shall be usurped."* [22]

This is the current situation, and citizens do not like it:

- 64% of Americans believe that government is too big (6% believe it is too small, and only 25% believe that it is "the right size"), and only 35% believe that the government is operating in line with the U. S. Constitution. [23]

- When asked to identify the biggest threat to the future of the country, 55% identified big government, 32% big business, and 10% big labor. [24]

- 70% of Americans favor "smaller government with fewer services and lower taxes" rather than "a more active government with more services and higher taxes." [25]

Given the current public sentiment, state nullification (also historically called interposition) holds forth the promise of being a silver bullet – a proverbial wooden stake that can be driven through the heart of what many see as a growing federal monster.

But is state nullification actually a solution? As noted by Sir Francis Bacon in 1625, there are times when a remedy can be worse than the disease; so is state nullification a constitutional remedy or a constitutional disease? The answer is unequivocally provided by an historical review of the attempted use of state nullification over the past two centuries.

Of those many attempts, the one most frequently invoked by today's nullification supporters is that which occurred during the John Adams presidency. Adams was a leader of the Federalist Party, generally seen as wanting to strengthen the power of the federal government. Thomas Jefferson, his Vice-President, was the acknowledged leader of Anti-Federalist Party (also called the Republicans), who wanted to see a small and limited federal government, with most power remaining with the states. During the Adams presidency (1797-1801), the Federalists were in ascendency, holding not only the presidency but also Congress; and probably the most notable event of the Adams presidency was the XYZ Affair.

During Washington's presidency (when John Adams was Vice-President), France and Great Britain had been at war, so Great Britain blockaded American ships coming to Europe, thus straining relations between Great Britain and America. In 1794, John Jay negotiated a treaty with the British (known as the Jay Treaty) to ease the growing tensions as well as settle disputes remaining from the American Revolution. When the Jay Treaty was ratified in 1796, the French (still at war with the British) responded by seizing 300 American ships bound for British ports.

In 1797, President Adams, in an attempt to prevent war, dispatched three diplomats to negotiate with French officials. But before the Americans were permitted to meet with those officials, French agents demanded as pre-conditions: (1) a formal apology from President Adams, (2) a $10-million low-interest loan to the French government, and (3) a $250,000 personal bribe to the French foreign minister, Charles Tallyrand. Of course, the Americans refused.

The French threatened an invasion of the United States and continued to seize American ships. Congress therefore authorized a military buildup and began preparations for war, but Adams' Anti-Federalist opponents believed he was exaggerating the situation and demanded proof of his claims. Adams released an official report, including the diplomatic correspondence in which the actual names of the French agents were withheld, being identified only as W, X, Y, and Z.

Americans were outraged, and while a formal declaration of war against France was narrowly averted, an unofficial naval war nevertheless occurred (now called the Quasi War), which lasted from 1797 until 1800. France eventually relented and signed a treaty with America in 1800.

One of the factors that had early exacerbated the tensions between America and France had been the unscrupulous effort of French citizens living in America (such as Edmond-Charles Genêt), who had worked against American government, attempting to stir up American citizens to bypass their government and become directly involved in the conflict between the French and British. In 1798 at the height of tensions between France and America, Congress passed four federal laws designed to control the activities of foreigners in America during a time of national danger and impending war. Those laws, known as the "Alien and Sedition Acts," included:

- **The Naturalization Act**, extending the residency period from 5 to 14 years for aliens seeking citizenship.
- **The Alien Friends Act**, allowing the expulsion of aliens deemed dangerous during peacetime.
- **The Alien Enemies Act**, allowing the expulsion or imprisonment of aliens from a country with which America was at war if those aliens were deemed dangerous.
- **The Sedition Act**, authorizing fines or imprisonment for individuals who issued "false, scandalous, and malicious writing" against the government or its officials, whether Congress or the president.

The Alien Acts were never enforced but the Sedition Act was, with twenty-five individuals being arrested, and ten convicted and imprisoned. Jefferson's Anti-Federalists saw this law as directly attacking them, for they had been openly critical of the president and Congress and most of those arrested and charged by Federalist sheriffs and judges had been Anti-Federalists.

(The Acts eventually caused the public to turn against the Federalists, greatly assisting in Jefferson and the Anti-Federalists taking control of government in 1801. When Jefferson became president, he immediately pardoned all those convicted under the Sedition Act. The Naturalization Act was repealed in 1802, and the other two acts were allowed to expire without having been used.)

During the height of the Anti-Federalist opposition to the Alien & Sedition Acts, Jefferson (Adams' Vice President) had secretly written for the legislature of Kentucky (a new state recently formed from the territorial holdings of Virginia) a resolution that condemned the Acts as unjust exercises of federal powers; [26] James Madison wrote a similar resolution for the Virginia legislature, [27] and the two resolutions were adopted by their respective legislatures. The Kentucky Resolution declared that the federal Alien & Sedition Acts were "altogether void and of no force; and that the power to create, define, and punish such other crimes is reserved and of right appertains solely and exclusively to the respective states, each within its own territory"; the Virginia Resolution similarly declared that "the acts aforesaid are unconstitutional." [28]

Modern nullification advocates invoke these Resolutions as today's precedent for individual states nullifying federal laws on issues such as health care, cap and trade, etc., but today's supporters omit the rest of the story about the Resolutions, and what is omitted is actually much more important than the part they tell.

Significantly, Virginia and Kentucky had not sought to act alone as individual states. To the contrary, they submitted their proposal to the other states for their approval and joint action. But the other states, upon receiving those nullification resolutions, soundly condemned them. Their explanations for rejecting them centered around three common concerns.

1. The proper authority for ascertaining the constitutionality of federal laws was federal courts, not *state* legislatures. As Vermont explained:

[T]he General Assembly of the State of Vermont do highly disapprove of the resolutions of the General Assembly of Virginia as being unconstitutional in their nature and dangerous in their tendency. It belongs not to state legislatures to decide

on the constitutionality of laws made by the general [federal] government, this power being exclusively vested in the judiciary courts of the Union. [29] (emphasis added)

(Similar declarations were made by other state legislatures. [30])

2. Such actions by state legislatures abrogate the federal election process set forth in the Constitution for expressing the "consent of the governed" at the national level; federal laws reflect the will of the majority of states while nullification reflects the will of only one, or a few states:

The Legislature of Massachusetts....deem it their duty solemnly to declare that while they hold sacred the principle that the consent of the people is the only pure source of just and legitimate power, they cannot admit the right of the state legislatures to denounce the administration of that [federal] government to which the people themselves, by a solemn compact [the Constitution], have exclusively committed their national concerns....That the people in that solemn compact (which is declared to be the supreme law of the land [Article VI, Paragraph 2 of the Constitution]), have not constituted the state legislatures the judges of the acts or measures of the federal government. [31]

(Other state legislatures expressed the same sentiments.) [32]

3. A phrase used by multiple state legislatures was that the Kentucky and Virginia Resolutions were "of a dangerous tendency." [33] Why? Because not only did they negate the "consent of the governed" at the federal level but they also set the precarious precedent of allowing a state to invalidate any federal law with which it disagreed, for any reason. As insightfully explained by the Massachusetts legislature:

[S]hould the respectable state of Virginia persist in the assumption of the right to declare the acts of the national government unconstitutional, and should she oppose successfully her force and will to those of the nation, the Constitution would be reduced to a mere cipher – to the form and pageantry of authority without the energy of power. Every act of the federal government which thwarted the views or checked the ambitious projects of a particular state or of its leading

and influential members would be the object of opposition and of remonstrance, while the people – convulsed and confused by the conflict between two hostile jurisdictions and enjoying the protection of neither – would be wearied into a submission to some bold leader who would establish himself on the ruins of both.[34]

While the Kentucky and Virginia resolutions did propose the right of the collective states to nullify a federal law with which they disagreed, the other states rejected that proposition, so the resolutions were dropped. (Significantly, as will be seen below, both Jefferson and Madison later denounced as unconstitutional any nullification attempt whereby a state, or small group of states, attempted to act individually against the expressed will of the other states enacted through the federal Congress.)

Significantly, Founding Fathers such as George Washington deplored the Virginia and Kentucky Resolutions, lamenting to Patrick Henry that they had been the action of "a certain party among us to disquiet the public mind…[and] set the people at variance with their government." [35] He specifically bemoaned that "the State of Virginia has taken the lead in this opposition," [36] but he did take consolation in the fact that the rest of the United States had rejected the measure, rejoicing that "in no state (except Kentucky, that I have heard of) has legislative countenance [approval] been obtained beyond Virginia." [37]

Yet the Virginia and Kentucky Resolutions were not the first (nor the last) attempt by a state or citizens to express their displeasure with a federal law by "nullifying" it. The first occurred during the presidency of George Washington.

In 1791, the federal government enacted a tax on whiskey as a means of helping pay down the national debt from the American Revolution. In 1794 when parts of Pennsylvania and Virginia revolted against that tax, President Washington personally led the military against them to demonstrate that the federal authority as constituted by all the states prevailed over the regional predilections of just one or two states. As Washington affirmed, America was "an indissoluble union of the states under one federal head" and that "the glorious fabric of our independency and national character must be supported." 38

According to Washington, it had been completely appropriate for him to "take measures" because the state rejection of a federal law was not only an action "employed in propagating principles of anarchy" but was also dangerous because the "government is set at defiance." 39 To Washington, the real issue was "whether a small portion of the United States shall dictate to the whole Union," 40 and the obvious answer was no, but this did not prevent further attempts. In fact, nullification attempts also occurred in reaction to federal laws passed under presidents Thomas Jefferson and James Madison.

During Jefferson's presidency, Great Britain (at war with France – again) not only illegally impressed American citizens as British sailors but also attacked an American ship at Norfolk, Virginia. Tensions between the two nations grew and negotiations ensued, but Secretary of State James Monroe was unable to reach a satisfactory agreement. In an effort to punish Great Britain as well as prevent American involvement in the Napoleonic Wars in Europe, Congress passed the Embargo Act of 1807, containing two major provisions: (1) American ships were banned from traveling to foreign ports (unless personally approved by President Jefferson); and (2) in order to ensure compliance with the first provision, American ships were required to post a bond equivalent to the value of the ship and cargo. This Act imposed such an economic hardship on American shipping that compliance was low; in 1808, Congress therefore passed a new embargo act requiring American ships to post a bond for double the value of the ship and cargo.

Those Acts were highly unpopular in New England, where shipping was the heart of their economy. Strangely, while those acts prohibited American ships from trading in foreign ports, foreign ships (including English ones) were free to come to American ports; the Acts therefore hurt American trade but helped British trade. The result of the Embargo Acts was an economic disaster that created a regional depression and produced extremely high unemployment in

New England. Attempting to circumvent those restrictions, American smuggling skyrocketed, so in early 1809, Congress passed the Enforcement Act, authorizing the military to enforce the federal Acts. The Massachusetts Legislature nullified the Enforcement Act, announcing that it was "not legally binding," but the issue became moot, for only three days before Jefferson left office, he repealed the acts.

Shortly after Madison became President in 1809, he signed the Non-Intercourse Act that validated Jefferson's repeals while maintaining the embargoes against Great Britain and France. Consequently, much of the problem continued, for Great Britain and France still enjoyed the benefits of trading in America without American shipping enjoying the same reciprocal benefits abroad. Discontent was thus kept alive in New England.

Furthermore, the tensions already existing between America and Great Britain increased, with the British offering direct assistance to Indians attacking Americans, interfering with American shipping to non-embargoed ports, and continuing to forcibly impress American citizens into the British navy. Unable to resolve these conflicts, in 1812 Congress called on governors to organize the state militias and then officially declared war.

Support for the War of 1812 was largely along party lines, with the Anti-Federalists generally supporting it and the Federalists generally opposing it. The Federalists even called it "Mr. Madison's War," blaming it on a string of inept government actions by the Anti-Federalists (i.e., the Republicans).

Massachusetts pledged its efforts to thwart every action of Congress relating to the war, declaring that it would not fight in any war where the state of Massachusetts had not been specifically attacked on its own soil. The Supreme Court of Massachusetts also announced that any state governor could nullify a declaration of war made by the federal government. Both Massachusetts and Connecticut withheld their state militias from being used to repel the British invasion.

President Madison specifically reprobated these actions in his 1812 address to Congress:

Among the incidents to the measures of the war, I am constrained to advert [turn attention] to the refusal of the governors of Massachusetts and Connecticut to furnish the required detachments of militia toward the defense of the maritime frontier. The refusal was founded on a novel and unfortunate exposition of the provisions of the Constitution relating to the militia. [41]

The war nevertheless continued, remaining extremely unpopular among Federalists. Therefore, late in the war in December 1814 and January 1815, a convention of twenty-six Federalist leaders from Massachusetts, Connecticut, Rhode Island, New Hampshire, and Vermont met in Hartford, Connecticut, to consider measures to limit the power of the Anti-Federalists. They specifically rejected secession but did: (1) propose a separate peace treaty between New England and Great Britain, (2) issue a report condemning "Mr. Madison's War," (3) make three direct demands on Congress, and (4) propose seven constitutional amendments, including one to change presidential elections so that presidents could serve only one term, and two consecutive presidents could not be elected from the same state [42] (Presidents Madison and Jefferson had both served two terms, had both been from Virginia, and were both viewed by the Federalists as enemies.)

Significantly, other states, such as South Carolina, denounced the efforts of the Hartford Convention as "traitorous." [43] Even ex-president John Adams (himself a Federalist) had deplored the Federalist nullification attempts, specifically denouncing the Hartford Convention as an "inquisition" just as wrong as had been the conduct of bloody Robespierre during the French Revolution. [44]

The War of 1812 ended shortly after the Hartford Convention, so none of its measures gained traction; nevertheless, citizens across New England strongly disapproved of its actions, thus ensuring the eventual and permanent demise of the Federalists as a political party.

Subsequent attempts at state nullification occurred during the 1820s, involving first Georgia, and then South Carolina. The Georgia attempt revolved around federal measures related to the protection of Indian tribes in the state.

During colonization, Georgia bought much of its lands from the Indians. In 1802, it ceded its claim to western territorial lands to the federal government in exchange for a cash payment and the United States agreeing to settle with the Indians all remaining claims to tribal lands in Georgia. Much progress was made by the federal government in this regard until about 1820, when several unscrupulous whites urged the Indians to create a separate state within Georgia.

Facing that internal threat, the Georgia legislature pushed President Monroe to finish settling Indian claims in Georgia, so in February 1825, just before he left office and using great pressure, he got the Indian chieftains to cede the remaining lands. When that treaty was ratified by the U. S. Senate, Georgia immediately began surveying the new lands, but the Indians resisted, claiming that the treaty had been improperly negotiated.

A number of the chiefs approached the new President, John Quincy Adams, asserting that the agreement had been fraudulently pressed upon them; the government's own federal Indian agent (who had been present at the signing of the previous treaty) agreed. President Adams therefore instructed Georgia to cease from surveying until the dispute was settled.

(Article I, Section 10 of the Constitution stipulates that only the federal government can negotiate treaties with Indian tribes, and Article VI, Paragraph 2 of the Constitution specifically makes those Indian treaties part of the "supreme law of the land," unequivocally placing them above state courts and state law.)

The governor refused to heed Adams' order and sought approval from the state legislature to resist the federal government with armed force. But when President Adams sent the U. S. military to Georgia, Georgia backed down.

In January 1826, a new agreement was signed with the Indians, this time with their full approval. The Adams administration then notified Georgia that all claims had been settled, but the U. S. Senator from Georgia claimed there was a million acres shortfall. The Georgia governor therefore ordered surveyors to include a million acres in their survey, but the Indians resisted the surveyors on that acreage and appealed again to President Adams.

Adams ordered federal marshals to arrest anyone caught surveying in that area. Significantly, the policy pursued by Adams was a policy which Thomas Jefferson had strongly approved. As Jefferson had explained:

[T]he Indians have a right to the occupation of their lands, independent of the states within whose chartered lines they happen to be – that until they cede them by treaty (or other transaction equivalent to a treaty), no act of a state can give a right to such lands; that under the Constitution. . . [no] state or person [has] a right to treat with the Indians without the consent of the general [federal] government; . . . that the government is determined to exert all its energy for the patronage and protection of the rights of the Indians . . . and that if any settlements are made on lands not ceded by them without the previous consent of the United States, the government will think itself bound not only to declare to the Indians that such settlements are without the authority or protection of the United States but to remove [the settlers] also by the public force. [45]

Nevertheless, the Georgia governor retaliated against Adams' order that federal marshals arrest offending parties by ordering all state law officers to arrest any federal marshal who attempted to arrest surveyors, and to release anyone arrested by the federal government. The governor also ordered the state militia to prepare to resist the threatened invasion of United States forces.

This time, it was President Adams who backed down. Georgia therefore moved forward, subjugating the Indians under Georgia jurisdiction or forcing them to leave the state. Georgia even ordered the imprisonment of the Rev. Samuel A. Worcester of Vermont, who lived among the Indians as a missionary. Worcester sued to the Supreme Court, who ruled in his favor and ordered his release, [46] but the governor declared that federal courts were incompetent to settle the matter and refused to obey the order. [47]

The Georgia attempt at nullification was the only attempt of the many nullification efforts to be partially successful, and that was only because President Adams had backed down.

South Carolina was the next to attempt nullification, focusing its opposition around three issues.

The first was that of slavery. In 1820, Congress passed the Missouri Compromise, attempting to conciliate southern pro-slavery interests with northern anti-slavery interests. The Missouri Compromise repealed the 1789 law (signed by George Washington) which had forbidden slavery in any federal territory; the new compromise allowed slavery to begin moving into certain federal territories while continuing to prohibit it in others. Yet contrary to the optimistic predictions made during the compromise, the law actually fueled the sectionalism already present by energizing abolition forces in the north to fight the spread of slavery into new territories that had previously forbidden it; the compromise thus further polarized the nation along political and regional lines.

The second issue was that of public lands and westward expansion. In 1820, Congress passed measures to encourage western settlement by reducing the price and minimum requirements for the purchase of western lands, but disagreement arose over how to disperse the proceeds received by the federal government for the sales of those lands. Henry Clay of Kentucky proposed distributing the proceeds from the sale of public lands to the states, but Thomas Hart Benton of Missouri proposed gradually reducing the price of land until the federal government simply gave it away.

The third issue was that of protective tariffs. In 1828, Congress passed a tariff bill to protect American industry from being driven out of business by lower priced European (and especially lower priced British) goods. (The 1828 bill, passed under President John Quincy Adams, was merely the continuation of an 1816 federal law that had been enacted for the "protection and encouragement of American industry." [48]) Critics claimed the 1828 law helped manufacturing interests (which predominated in the northeast) but not agricultural ones (which predominated throughout the south).

In 1829 after Andrew Jackson became President and John C. Calhoun Vice-President, a Senator Samuel Foot of Connecticut proposed that the sale of federal lands in the west be halted. Senator Benton claimed that this was just another attempt to help northeastern manufacturing states by keeping their workers from moving west, which would raise their manufacturing costs. Benton's claim prompted Senator Robert Hayne of South Carolina to call for an alliance of southern and western states to join against the northeast. He urged state nullification of any federal law they believed would weaken their interests.

In late January 1830, Senator Daniel Webster of Massachusetts responded to Hayne with one of the most famous speeches and recognizable lines in American history. In a debate that lasted more than a week on the Senate floor, Webster pointed out that the United States was not just a confederation of states but instead was the creation of the people, and that the people had placed ultimate power and sovereignty in the Constitution and in the federal government it had created. Webster, like the Founders before him, argued that if a state disapproved an action of the federal government, it had a right to seek redress in federal court or to amend the Constitution, but it had no constitutional right simply to nullify a federal law – that to do so would produce anarchy and eventually could result in a sectional or a civil war. In fact, he predicted that nullification would cause the Union to dissolve and that the American flag, "drenched...in fraternal blood," would wave over "the broken and dishonored fragments of our once glorious empire." [49] Webster then proclaimed the famous words that were to resound throughout history – that it was wrong to think that Americans could have "liberty first, and union afterwards," but that the proper view was "Liberty and Union – now and forever, one and inseparable." [50]

Hayne's promotion of nullification led to a fissure between President Andrew Jackson and Vice President John C. Calhoun. In fact, in April 1830, only weeks after Webster's debate against Hayne, Jackson and Calhoun directly contradicted each other in public over the issue. In 1831, President Jackson reorganized his cabinet to rid himself of Calhoun supporters, and in 1832, Calhoun resigned as vice-president to become U. S. Senator from South Carolina.

From that point, South Carolina set itself vigorously to oppose any measure that it felt strengthened the federal government and actively sought an opportunity to invoke nullification, finally choosing the protective tariff as the focal point of its attack.

Attempting to lay groundwork for the upcoming fight, Calhoun invoked the Kentucky and Virginia Resolutions, explaining:

This right of interposition, thus solemnly asserted by the State of Virginia, be called what it may – state right, veto, nullification, or by any other name – I conceive to be the fundamental principle of our system. [51]

However, Calhoun went well beyond what had been proposed by Virginia and Kentucky, for rather than proposing that all the states unite in opposition, he asserted that if only one state "vetoed" any federal law, then that federal law could become valid only through a constitutional amendment ratified by three-fourths of the other states. Thus, according to Calhoun, the opinion of one state could be overridden only by three-fourths of the other states – and then, only through a constitutional amendment.

South Carolina's attack on the federal government finally came in 1832, and ironically, it came after Congress passed a bill lowering the protective tariff of 1828. (The revenue generated by the sale of western lands combined with the receipts received from the 1828 tariff generated enough income that the national debt was completely retired for the first time in American history; so because the government had its first-ever surplus, it had moved to lessen government income by reducing tariffs.) Even though the 1832 bill lowered the tariff, it still preserved the theory of protection, and since South Carolina believed the manufacturing states were the primary beneficiaries, it declared the tariff bills of both 1828 and 1832 null and void; [52] it even raised an army to defend its assertion of nullification. [53]

John C. Calhoun, who had become the national evangelist for the resurrected maldoctrine of nullification, also may have been the first prominent historical revisionist, for he had deliberately rewritten American history by claiming that nullification and state supremacy over the federal government was approved by the Founding Fathers – a claim disproved, ironically, even by the Founding Fathers of Calhoun's own state. David Franklin Houston (1866-1940), a noted academic who graduated from the University of South Carolina and who led five major universities during his life, accurately pointed out:

> *Charles Pinckney, Charles Cotesworth Pinckney, John Rutledge, and Pierce Butler were South Carolina's delegates to the Constitutional Convention. Of these, the two Pinckneys and Rutledge were decidedly in favor of establishing a strong national government capable of effectively executing its acts and of dispensing its benefits and protection. The two Pinckneys could scarcely find language sufficiently forcible to express their condemnation of the doctrine that the states were separately and individually sovereign. The entire delegation…advocated making the acts of Congress the supreme law of the several states [see Elliot, Debates, IV. 301]….Such sentiments were not only expressed in the Constitutional Convention but were also uttered with even more emphasis in the [South Carolina] State [Ratification] Convention itself….Charles Cotesworth Pinckney boldly proclaimed that attempts to weaken the Union by pretending that each state was separately and individually independent were political heresies which would produce serious distress. "The separate independence and individual sovereignty of the several states was never thought of by the enlightened band of patriots who framed this declaration [i.e., the Constitution]"* [Elliot, *Debates*, IV. 301]. [54]

Calhoun (and others) who wrongly asserted that the theory of nullification was valid did so because they viewed the United States not as a nation per se but rather only as a voluntary and temporary loosely knit association of individually sovereign states that had a right to nullify within its own state boundaries any actions of the federal government with which it disagreed. While Calhoun claimed this was the view of the Founding Fathers, it definitely was not – a point made especially clear in the *Federalist Papers* (penned by leading Founding Fathers John Jay, Alexander Hamilton, and James Madison). As explained by Houston:

> *A careful reading of the Federalist – a rational comparison of its various parts – reveals as to essential matters a consistent body of principles in support of the proposition that the States were not, when the Constitution was framed, and had never been, separate and independent sovereigns. There would be little disposition to question the correctness of this statement so far as Jay and Hamilton are concerned. If, however, confirmation were wanted as to Madison's views, it would be necessary only to refer to his expressions in the Constitutional Convention itself. Language could scarcely be more explicit. "Some contend that the States are sovereign, when in fact they are only political societies. There is a gradation of power in all societies, from the lowest corporation to the highest sovereign. The States never possessed the essential rights of sovereigns. These were always vested in Congress. Their voting as States in Congress is no evidence of sovereignty. The State of Maryland voted by counties. Did this make counties sovereign? The States, at present, are only great corporations, having the power of making by-laws, and these are effective only if they are not contradictory to the general [Union]."...Madison, with Jay and Hamilton, contended that even under the Confederation a Union existed which could exercise powers that no State could legally obstruct – a Union whose bonds no State could legally throw off. The authors of the Federalist speak not of establishing a union, but of preserving the Union and of the evils that would result from its dismemberment.* [55]

Returning to South Carolina, following its 1832 action to raise an army to enforce its nullification decision, President Jackson declared nullification illegal [56] and sought congressional approval to use force to ensure that federal law was executed. [57] Congress agreed and promptly passed a Force Act, under which Jackson dispatched the military to Charleston, South Carolina.

President Jackson, unlike President John Quincy Adams before him, was definitely not going to back down, so in 1833, Senator Henry Clay of Kentucky (who had misguidedly engineered the Missouri Compromise of 1820) sought to engineer a compromise between the United States and South Carolina to reduce the fever-pitched tensions between the two. Clay persuaded Congress to further reduce the tariffs, and so South Carolina rescinded its nullification ordinance against the tariff bills (but it then belligerently and defiantly adopted an ordinance nullifying the Force Act).

One of the most notable commentators on this national crisis was an elderly President James Madison, who recorded his observations in his lengthy "Notes on Nullification." [58] To help observers understand the beliefs associated with the maldoctrine of state nullification (or interposition), he recommended:

> *That [if] the doctrine of nullification may be clearly understood, it must be taken as laid down in the report of a special committee of the House of Representatives of S. C. in 1828. In that document it is asserted that a single state has a constitutional right to arrest the execution of a law of the U. S. within its limits – that the arrest is to be presumed right and valid and is to remain in force unless ¾ of the states, in a convention, shall otherwise decide.* [59]

Madison then unequivocally condemned nullification, noting that "a more fatal inlet to anarchy cannot be imagined" and that nullification was "a deadly poison" to the Constitution. [60] He especially denounced South Carolina's attempts to invoke his own Virginia Resolution and Jefferson's Kentucky Resolution as the basis of state nullification efforts:

> *The true question therefore is whether there be a constitutional right in a single state to nullify a law of the U. S. We have seen the absurdity of such a claim in its naked and suicidal form….The amount of this modified right of nullification is that a single state may arrest the operation of a law of the United States and institute a process which is to terminate in the ascendancy of a minority over a*

large majority in a republican system – the characteristic rule of which is that the majority will is the ruling will! And this newfangled theory is attempted to be fathered on Mr. Jefferson – the Apostle of Republicanism – and whose own words declare that "acquiescence in the decision of the majority is the vital principle of it [i.e., constitutional republicanism]." [61] (emphasis added)

John Quincy Adams agreed, and further added that nullification was used for a "monstrous and horrible object" [62] and that it was "portentous and fatal...to the prospect and welfare of this Union." [63] Madison and Adams thus joined the presidents before them (George Washington, John Adams, and Thomas Jefferson) in denouncing state nullification.

When President Andrew Jackson retired, he looked back over the nullification crisis and first praised the Constitution and then forcefully repudiated the maldoctrine of nullification:

These cheering and grateful prospects and these multiplied favors we owe, under Providence, to the adoption of the Federal Constitution. It is no longer a question whether this great country can remain happily united and flourish under our present form of government....But in order to maintain the Union unimpaired it is absolutely necessary that the laws passed by the constituted authorities should be faithfully executed in every part of the country, and that every good citizen should at all times stand ready to put down, with the combined force of the nation, every attempt at unlawful resistance under whatever pretext it may be made or whatever shape it may assume....It is impossible that any government can continue to exist upon any other principles. It would cease to be a government and be unworthy of the name if it had not the power to enforce the execution of its own laws within its own sphere of action. [64]

It was significant that <u>no</u> other state – not even any other southern state – stood with South Carolina in its belligerent refusal to follow the rule of federal law. After all, every measure South Carolina protested had been legitimately passed by the <u>entire</u> Congress through the process directed by the Constitution; it was simply that South Carolina disagreed with the result. In fact, in 1851 after the abolition movement began to spread into all quarters of the nation following the passage of the 1850 Fugitive Slave Law, South Carolina even urged secession, but no other state would join her at that time. It was not until after the election of 1860 when Republicans gained both the presidency and the Congress that the other ardent pro-slavery states saw the proverbial handwriting on the wall regarding abolition and thus joined together in secession. [65]

But secession came as no surprise, for it was merely the mature fruit produced by the anarchic maldoctrine of nullification. And secession, just like state nullification, had been deplored by the Framers. As Thomas Jefferson had early declared:

> *I fear, from an expression in your letter, that the people of Kentucky think of separating not only from Virginia [i.e., to become a separate state] (in which they are right), but also from the [United States]. I own I should think this a most calamitous event and such a one as every good citizen should set himself against.* [66] (emphasis added)

Jefferson expressed the same position against secession during the discussions over the Alien & Sedition Acts; [67] and during the War of 1812 when talk of secession was again raised, Jefferson repeated his condemnation.

Other Founders similarly deplored secession, including George Washington, [68] James Madison, [69] Alexander Hamilton, [70] and many others. But the Framers not only denounced secession but they also recognized that it proceeded from the maldoctrine of state nullification and hyper state sovereignty.

With the close of the Civil War, it was widely believed that the maldoctrine of nullification had finally and permanently been put to rest. However, such was not the case. In fact, in 1954 when the U. S. Supreme Court struck down desegregation in *Brown v. Board of Education*, [71] eight southern states invoked nullification (i.e., interposition), including Louisiana. [72] In 1960 when the Louisiana case reached the Supreme Court, the Court ruled "that interposition [nullification] is not a constitutional doctrine. If taken seriously, it is illegal defiance of constitutional authority" [73] (emphasis added). Yet now, fifty years later, this reprehensible maldoctrine is once again being resurrected.

The frustration behind modern nullification talk can be easily understood; and even though many may sympathize with its overall objectives, every citizen who loves his country and his Constitution must renounce, reject, and oppose this maldoctrine, boldly confronting it in every venue where it raises its venomous head.

Nullification is the hallmark of selfishness and anarchy; and selfishness and anarchy, whether by citizens or states, is not a cherished American virtue. To the contrary, a characteristic of America's greatness has been an unwavering dedication not only to follow the rule of law but also to expend as much time and energy necessary, no matter how long it takes, to make needed changes through the constitutional process, whether by the use of courts or through elections. While this is admittedly a much slower process, there is never an end-around for doing what is right, nor can right be secured by pursuing wrong.

(As an aside, there are some *constitutional* efforts being made to nullify – or remove the effects of – federal law, but these legitimate efforts are quite different from the state nullification movement. For example, many of the effects of the federal *Roe v. Wade* policy are being "nullified" through the passage of parental consent, informed consent, ultrasound, and other pro-life laws. Similarly, many states are passing laws that "nullify" the effects of federal gun control laws. Other states are pursuing action in federal courts to "nullify" healthcare, cap & trade, etc. All of these measures are praiseworthy and are quite different from the currently emerging nullification movement.)

So, in reviewing the history of the maldoctrine of state nullification, there have been several attempts to invoke this practice, and in each case, it was the attempt of a minority group to thwart the decision of the majority of states as enacted through the federal

Congress. George Washington explained why this was always an improper response:

> [T]he fundamental principle of our Constitution...enjoins [requires] that the will of the majority shall prevail. [74]

It was for the same constitutional reason that John Quincy Adams condemned nullification:

Democracy is self-government of the community by the conjoint will of the majority of numbers. What communion – what affinity can there be – between that principle and nullification?...Never – never was amalgamation so preposterous and absurd as that of nullification and democracy! [75]

While the losing side may sincerely believe that a law passed by Congress is unconstitutional, that opinion does not authorize them to pick and choose which federal laws they will obey. In fact, if the proposed policy of state nullification were to take hold today, the results would be completely inane. Consider, for example, that if Congress passed a law to <u>encourage</u> offshore drilling by states, a state such as Connecticut would nullify it; but if Congress passed a law <u>prohibiting</u> offshore drilling by states, then Alaska would likely nullify it. Similarly:

- A federal law <u>enforcing</u> prohibitions against illegal immigration would likely be nullified by California, but a law <u>easing</u> immigration restrictions would be nullified by Oklahoma.

- A federal law <u>increasing</u> gun control restrictions would be nullified by Arizona, but a law <u>easing</u> gun control restrictions would be nullified by Illinois.

- A mandatory climate-change cap and trade law would be nullified by Texas, but one permitting state options would be nullified by Minnesota.

- A law to protect marriage as the union of one man and one woman would be nullified by Massachusetts, but a law granting full partnership rights to homosexuals would be nullified by Alabama.

- A federal law banning abortion would be nullified by New York, but a law expanding abortion would be nullified by South Dakota.

There will always be a losing side on <u>every</u> federal law, and some state will always disagree with every law passed, but under nullification, the losing side would always win.

The losing side in any federal issue has two constitutional recourses available: (1) it can attempt to convince a majority of the nation that the law is unconstitutional and they can then remedy that law with a corrective measure in Congress (see *Federalist* #44 [76]) – as was done in many of the cases above; or (2) it can seek to have the federal law declared unconstitutional by the federal courts.

Whenever the minority loses to the majority, the proper response was set forth by Samuel Adams who, like all others, at times found himself on the losing side of an issue:

[A]s it becomes a citizen, I will acquiesce in the choice of a majority of the people. [77]

Nullification places minority power above majority power. The majority may sometimes be wrong, but when that occurs, Washington reminded Americans that changes must be made <u>only</u> by using "the way which the Constitution designates. But let there be no change by usurpation; for though this in one instance may be the instrument of good, it is the customary weapon by which free governments are destroyed." [78] Very simply, don't try to fix the Constitution by breaking it; fix the Constitution through the means it provides, and nullification is <u>not</u> that means. Nullification is a dangerous anarchic maldoctrine, cancerous and toxic to the health and vigor of a constitutional republic.

Endnotes for Appendix

1. "How the Senators Voted on Impeachment," *CNN*, February 12, 1999 (at: http://www.cnn.com/ALLPOLITICS/stories/1999/02/12/senate.vote/), which shows the votes 55-45 against the perjury charge and a split decision (50-50) on the obstruction of justice charge. See also "About President Clinton," *The History Place* (http://www.historyplace.com/unitedstates/impeachments/clinton.htm) (accessed February 8, 2010).

2. "About President Clinton," *The History Place* (at: http://www.historyplace.com/unitedstates/impeachments/clinton.htm) (accessed February 8, 2010).

3. "About President Clinton," *The History Place* (at: http://www.historyplace.com/unitedstates/impeachments/clinton.htm) (accessed February 8, 2010).

4. Debra Medina, "State Sovereignty," October 28, 2009, *MedinaForTexas.com* (at: http://www.medinafortexas.com/restoreSovereignty.php) (accessed January 29, 2010); see similar nullification comments in Debra Medina, "Protecting Texas-Gun Ownership," October 2, 2009, *MedinaForTexas.com* (at: http://www.medinafortexas.com/gunOwnership.php) (accessed January 29, 2010); see also Christy Hoppe, "Debra Medina Says Texas Should Ignore Some U.S. Treaties," January 12, 2010, *Trailblazersblog.DallasNews.com* (at: http://trailblazersblog.dallasnews.com/archives/2010/01/debra-medina-says-texas-should.html) (accessed January 29, 2010).

5. "Ron Paul on the Mike Church Show," *RonPaul.com*, December 10, 2009 (at: http://www.ronpaul.com/2009-12-10/ron-paul-on-the-mike-church-show/).

6. Thomas Jefferson, *Writings of Thomas Jefferson*, Albert Ellery Bergh, editor (Washington, D. C.: The Thomas Jefferson Memorial Association, 1904), Vol. III, p. 146, "Opinion Against the Constitutionality of a National Bank," February 15, 1791.

7. Thomas Jefferson, *Writings of Thomas Jefferson*, Albert Ellery Bergh, editor (Washington, D. C.: The Thomas Jefferson Memorial Association, 1904), Vol. XV, pp. 448-451, letter to Judge William Johnson, June 12, 1823.

8. Thomas Jefferson, *Writings of Thomas Jefferson*, Albert Ellery Bergh, editor (Washington, D. C.: The Thomas Jefferson Memorial Association, 1904), Vol. X, p. 167, letter to Gideon Granger, August 13, 1800.

9. Jonathan Elliott, *The Debates in the Several State Conventions on the Adoption of the Federal Constitution* (Washington, 1836), Vol. IV, p. 428, James Madison on "The Cod Fishery Bill," February 7, 1792.

10. Jonathan Elliott, *The Debates in the Several State Conventions on the Adoption of the Federal Constitution* (Washington, 1836), Vol. IV, p. 429, James Madison on "The Cod Fishery Bill," February 7, 1792.

11.Joseph Story, *Commentaries on the Constitution of the United States* (Boston: Hilliard, Gray, and Company, 1833), Book III, pp. 712-713, Chapter XLIV, § 1009-1010. Joseph Story, *Commentaries on the Constitution of the United States* (Boston: Charles C. Little and James Brown, 1851), Vol. II, pp. 612- 613, §1907-1908.

12. Samuel Adams, *The Writings of Samuel Adams*, Harry Alonzo Cushing, editor (New York: G. P. Putnam's Sons, 1908), Vol. IV, pp. 330-332, letter to Elbridge Gerry, August 22, 1789.

13. Jonathan Elliot, *The Debates in the Several State Conventions on the Adoption of the Federal Constitution* (Washington, 1836), Vol. III, pp. 149-150, Patrick Henry, June 7, 1788; Vol. III, pp. 156, 161, 174, Patrick Henry, June 9, 1788, at the Virginia Ratifying Convention for the U. S. Constitution.

14. John Elliot, *The Debates in the Several State Conventions on the Adoption of the Federal Constitution* (Washington, 1836), Vol. III, pp. 271- 272, George Mason, June 11, 1788, at the Virginia Ratification Convention for the U. S. Constitution.

15. Jonathan Elliot, *The Debates in the Several State Conventions on the Adoption of the Federal Constitution* (Washington, 1836), Vol. II, pp. 456-457, 481- 482, James Wilson, December 4, 1787, at the Pennsylvania Ratification Convention for the U. S. Constitution.

16. Max Farrand, *The Records of the Federal Convention of 1787* (New Haven: Yale University Press, 1911), Vol. I, pp. 165-166, June 8, 1787; Vol. II, p. 317, August 17, 1787; Vol. II, p. 362, August 21, 1787; etc., Elbridge Gerry speaking at the Constitutional Convention.

17. Jonathan Elliot, *The Debates in the Several State Conventions on the Adoption of the Federal Constitution* (Washington, 1836), Vol. II, pp. 537- 538, 540, Thomas M'Kean, December 11, 1787.

18. Jonathan Elliot, *The Debates in the Several State Conventions on the Adoption of the Federal Constitution* (Washington, 1836), Vol. III, p. 186, Richard Henry Lee, June 9, 1788, at the Virginia Ratification Convention for the U. S. Constitution.

19. Max Farrand, *The Records of the Federal Convention of 1787* (New Haven: Yale University Press, 1911), Vol. III, p. 284, Luther Martin's Reply to the Landholder [Oliver Ellsworth], March 14, 1788; and Vol. III, pp. 286-287, Luther Martin's Reply to the Landholder [Oliver Ellsworth], March 19, 1788; and Vol. III, p. 295-296, Luther Martin's Letter to the Citizens of Maryland, March 25, 1788.

20. James D. Richardson, *Messages and Papers of the Presidents* (Washington, D. C.: Government Printing Office, 1899), Vol. II, pp. 152- 155, James Monroe, "Views of the President of the United States on the Subject of Internal Improvements," May 4, 1822.

21. Samuel Adams, *The Writings of Samuel Adams*, Harry Alonzo Cushing, editor (New York: G. P. Putnam's Sons, 1906), Vol. II, p. 287, Article Signed "Candidus," originally printed in the Boston Gazette, December 9, 1771.

22. Thomas Jefferson, *Writings of Thomas Jefferson*, Albert Ellery Bergh, editor (Washington D. C.: Thomas Jefferson Memorial Association, 1904), Vol. XV, pp. 331-332, to Charles Hammond on August 18, 1821.

23. "New Judicial Watch-SurveyUSA Poll Shows Deep Divide between Obama Administration and Likely Voters on Wide Range of Issues," *Judicial Watch*, December 11-14, 2009 (at: http://www.judicialwatch.org/news/2009/dec/new-judicial-watch-surveyusa-poll-shows-deep-divide-between-obama-administration-and-l).

24. "Big Gov't. Still Viewed as Greater Threat Than Big Business," *Gallup*, April 20, 2009 (at: http://www.gallup.com/poll/117739/Big-Gov-Viewed-Greater-Threat-Big-Business.aspx).

25. "America's Best Days," *Rasmussen Poll*, December 17, 2009 (results from August 2009)(at:http://www.rasmussenreports.com/public_content/politics/mood_of_america/ameri ca_s_best_days).

26. Thomas Jefferson, *The Papers of Thomas Jefferson* (Princeton: Princeton University Press, 2003), Vol. 30, pp. 536-543, Jefferson's Draft of the Kentucky Resolutions, before October 4, 1798; *Papers of Thomas Jefferson* (2003), Vol. 30, pp. 543-549, Jefferson's Fair

Copy, before October 4, 1798; Papers of Thomas Jefferson (2003), Vol. 30, pp. 550-556, "Resolutions Adopted by the Kentucky General Assembly," November 10, 1798.

27. Jonathan Elliott, *The Debates in the Several State Conventions on the Adoption of the Federal Constitution* (Washington, 1836), Vol. IV, pp. 528-529, "Virginia Resolutions of 1798," December 21, 1798.

28. Thomas Jefferson, *The Papers of Thomas Jefferson* (Princeton: Princeton University Press, 2003), Vol. 30, p. 550, "Resolutions Adopted by the Kentucky General Assembly," November 10, 1798, Jonathan Elliott, *The Debates in the Several State Conventions on the Adoption of the Federal Constitution* (Washington, 1836), Vol. IV, pp. 528-529, "Virginia Resolutions of 1798," December 21, 1798.

29. Jonathan Elliott, *The Debates in the Several State Conventions on the Adoption of the Federal Constitution* (Washington, 1836), Vol. IV, p. 539, The Vermont House of Representatives, October 30, 1799.

30. See, for example, Jonathan Elliott, *The Debates in the Several State Conventions on the Adoption of the Federal Constitution* (Washington, 1836), Vol. IV, pp. 532, 537-539, declarations from the New Hampshire House of Representatives, June 14, 1799; the New York Senate, March 5, 1799; the Delaware House of Representatives, February 1, 1799; etc.

31. Jonathan Elliott, *The Debates in the Several State Conventions on the Adoption of the Federal Constitution* (Washington, 1836), Vol. IV, pp. 533-534, The Massachusetts Senate, February 9, 1799.

32. See, for example, Jonathan Elliott, *The Debates in the Several State Conventions on the Adoption of the Federal Constitution* (Washington, 1836), Vol. IV, pp. 537-538, the New York Senate, March 5, 1799.

33. Jonathan Elliott, *The Debates in the Several State Conventions on the Adoption of the Federal Constitution* (Washington, 1836), Vol. IV, pp. 532, 539, Delaware House of Representatives, February 1, 1799; Vermont House of Representatives, October 30, 1799; etc.

34. Jonathan Elliott, *The Debates in the Several State Conventions on the Adoption of the Federal Constitution* (Washington, 1836), Vol. IV, p. 534, The Massachusetts Senate, February 9, 1799.

35. George Washington, *The Writings of George Washington*, John C. Fitzpatrick, editor (Washington, D. C.: U. S. Government Printing Office, 1940), Vol. 37, p. 87, letter to Patrick Henry, January 15, 1799.

36. George Washington, *The Writings of George Washington*, John C. Fitzpatrick, editor (Washington, D. C.: U. S. Government Printing Office, 1940), Vol. 37, p. 87, letter to Patrick Henry, January 15, 1799.

37. George Washington, *The Writings of George Washington*, John C. Fitzpatrick, editor (Washington, D. C.: U. S. Government Printing Office, 1940), Vol. 37, pp. 87- 88, letter to Patrick Henry, January 15, 1799.

38. George Washington, *The Last Official Address of His Excellency General Washington to the Legislatures of the United States, to Which is Annexed a Collection of Papers Relative to Half-Pay, and Commutation of Half-Pay Granted by Congress to the Officers of the Army* (Hartford: Hudson and Goodwin, 1783), p. 6.

39. George Washington, *The Addresses and Messages of the Presidents of the United States, from 1789 to 1839* (New York: McLean and Taylor, 1839), p. 53, Proclamation, September 25, 1794.

40. George Washington, *The Addresses and Messages of the Presidents of the United States,*

from 1789 to 1839 (New York: McLean and Taylor, 1839), p. 53, Proclamation, September 25, 1794.

41. James Madison, *The Writings of James Madison, Comprising His Public Papers and His Private Correspondence, Including Numerous Letters and Documents Now For the First Time Printed*, Gaillard Hunt, editor (New York:.G. P. Putnam's Sons, 1908), Vol. VIII, p. 224, Fourth Annual Message to Congress, November 4, 1812.

42. "Amendments to the Constitution Proposed by the Hartford Convention," *The Avalon Project*, 1814 (at: http://avalon.law.yale.edu/19th_century/hartconv.asp).

43. David Franklin Houston, *A Critical Study of Nullification in South Carolina* (New York: Longman, Greens and Co., 1896), p. 25; citing David R. Williams, *Charleston Mercury*, August 27, 1828.

44. John Adams, *The Works of John Adams, Second President of the United States: With A Life of the Author, Notes and Illustrations*, Charles Francis Adams, editor (Boston: Charles C. Little and James Brown, 1851), Vol. VI, p. 403.

45. Thomas Jefferson, *The Writings of Thomas Jefferson*, Andrew A. Lipscomb, editor (Washington, D.C.: The Thomas Jefferson Memorial Association, 1903), Vol. VIII, pp. 226-227, letter to General Knox, August 10, 1791. *See also* George Tucker, *The Life of Thomas Jefferson; Third President of the United States; With Parts of His Correspondence Never Before Published, and Notices of His Opinions On Questions of Civil Government, National Policy, and Constitutional Law* (London: Charles Knight and Co., 1837), Vol. I, pp. 400-401, Thomas Jefferson in a letter to General Knox.

46. *Worcester v. Georgia*, 31 U. S. 515 (1832).

47. John W. Burgess, *American History Series: The Middle Period, 1817-1858* (New York: Charles Scribner's Sons, 1897), p. 219.

48. John Quincy Adams, *Address of John Quincy Adams, To His Constituents of the Twelfth Congressional District, At Braintree, September 17th, 1842* (Boston: J. H. Eastburn, Printer, 1842), p. 8.

49. Daniel Webster, *Speeches of Hayne and Webster In the United States Senate, on the Resolution of Mr. Foot, January, 1830* (Boston: Redding and Company, 1852), p. 84.

50. Daniel Webster, *Speeches of Hayne and Webster In the United States Senate, on the Resolution of Mr. Foot, January, 1830* (Boston: Redding and Company, 1852), p. 84.

51. John C. Calhoun, "The Fort Hill Address: On the Relations of the States and Federal Government," *Online Library of Liberty*, July 26, 1831 (at: http://oll.libertyfund.org/title/683/107120).

52. "South Carolina Ordinance of Nullification," *The Avalon Project*, November 24, 1832 (at: http://avalon.law.yale.edu/19th_century/ordnull.asp).

53. Andrew Jackson, "President Jackson's Proclamation Regarding Nullification," *Avalon Project*, December 10, 1832 (at: http://avalon.law.yale.edu/19th_century/jack01.asp), where he says "This, then, is the position in which we stand. A small majority of the citizens of one State in the Union, have elected delegates to the State Convention: that Convention has ordained, that all the revenue laws of the United States, must be repealed, or that they are no longer a member of the Union. The Governor of that State has recommended to the Legislature the raising of an army to carry the secession into effect, and that he may be empowered to give clearances to vessels in the name of the State."

54. David Franklin Houston, *A Critical Study of Nullification in South Carolina* (New York: Longman, Greens and Co., 1896), pp. 26-27.

55. David Franklin Houston, *A Critical Study of Nullification in South Carolina* (New York:

Longman, Greens and Co., 1896), pp. 17-18.

56. Andrew Jackson, "President Jackson's Proclamation Regarding Nullification," *The Avalon Project*, December 10, 1832 (at:
http://avalon.law.yale.edu/19th_century/jack01.asp).

57. Andrew Jackson, "President Jackson's Proclamation Regarding Nullification," *The Avalon Project*, December 10, 1832 (at:
http://avalon.law.yale.edu/19th_century/jack01.asp).

58. James Madison, *The Writings of James Madison*, Gaillard Hunt, editor (New York: G. P. Putnam's Sons, 1910), Vol. IX, pp. 573-607, "Notes on Nullification," 1835-1836; these notes were written almost entirely in Madison's own hand and revised by him with the aid of Mrs. Madison and his brother-in-law, John C. Payne.

59. James Madison, *The Writings of James Madison*, Gaillard Hunt, editor (New York: G. P. Putnam's Sons, 1910), Vol. IX, p. 573, "Notes on Nullification,"1835-1836.

60. James Madison, *The Writings of James Madison*, Gaillard Hunt, editor (New York: G. P. Putnam's Sons, 1910), Vol. IX, pp. 575-578, "Notes on Nullification,"1835-1836.

61. James Madison, *The Writings of James Madison*, Gaillard Hunt, editor (New York: G. P. Putnam's Sons, 1910), Vol. IX, pp. 588-589, "Notes on Nullification,"1835-1836.

62. John Quincy Adams, *Address of John Quincy Adams, To His Constituents of the Twelfth Congressional District, At Braintree, September 17th, 1842* (Boston: J. H. Eastburn, Printer, 1842), p. 8.

63. John Quincy Adams, *Address of John Quincy Adams, To His Constituents of the Twelfth Congressional District, At Braintree, September 17th, 1842* (Boston: J. H. Eastburn, Printer, 1842), p. 10.

64. Andrew Jackson, "Farewell Address, March 4, 1837," *American Presidency Project Online* (at: http://www.presidency.ucsb.edu/ws/?pid=67087) (accessed January 14, 2010).

65. While many southern apologists today argue that the slavery issue had nothing to do with secession, the secession documents of the southern seceding states prove exactly the opposite – that imminent abolition was the cause of their secession. To see these documents, go to "Confronting Civil War Revisionism: Why the South Went to War" (at: http://www.wallbuilders.com/LIBissuesArticles.asp?id=92).

66. Thomas Jefferson, *The Works of Thomas Jefferson*, Paul Leicester Ford, editor (New York: G.P. Putnam's Sons, 1904), Vol. V, pp. 74-75, letter to Archibald Stuart, January 25, 1786.

67. Thomas Jefferson, *The Works of Thomas Jefferson*, Paul Leicester Ford, editor (New York: G.P. Putnam's Sons, 19054), Vol. VIII, letter to John Taylor, June 1, 1798; and Vol. VII, p. 390, letter to Wilson C. Nicholas, September 5, 1799.

68. George Washington, *The Writings of George Washington*, John C. Fitzpatrick, editor (Washington, D. C.: Government Printing Office, 1938), Vol. 26, pp. 483-496, Circular to the States, June 8, 1783.

69. William C. Rives, *History of the Life and Times of James Madison* (Boston: Little, Brown, and Company, 1866), pp. 626-628, correspondence between Alexander Hamilton and James Madison concerning possible secession or receding from the constitutional compact, Saturday and Sunday, July 1788.

70. Alexander Hamilton, *The Papers of Alexander Hamilton*, Harold C. Syrett, editor (New York: Columbia University Press, 1979), Vol. XXVI, p. 309, letter to Theodore Sedgwick, July 10, 1804.

71. *Brown v. Board of Education of Topeka*, 347 U.S. 483 (1954).

72. See, for example, *Educational Freedom in Urban America: Brown v. Board after Half a Century*, David Salisbury and Casey Lartigue Jr., editors (Washington, D. C.: Cato Institute, 2004), p. 18; "Timeline of Events Leading to the *Brown v. Board of Education* Decision, 1954," *National Archives* (at: http://www.archives.gov/education/lessons/brown-v-board/timeline.html) (accessed February 9, 2010); *The Doctrine of Interposition: Its History and Application. A Report on Senate Joint Resolution 3, General Assembly of Virginia, 1956, and Related Matters* (Commonwealth of Virginia: 1957) (at: http://www2.vcdh.virginia.edu/civilrightstv/documents/images/DoctrineInterposition.pdf); the eight states were Alabama, Arkansas, Florida, Georgia, Louisiana, Mississippi, South Carolina, and Virginia.

73. *Bush v. Orleans Parish School Board*, 364 U.S. 500, Justia.com, 1960 (at: http://supreme.justia.com/us/364/500/case.html).

74. James D. Richardson, *Messages and Papers of the Presidents* (Washington, D. C.: Government Printing Office, 1897), Vol. I, p. 156, George Washington's "Sixth Annual Address" of November 19, 1794.

75. John Quincy Adams, *Address of John Quincy Adams, To His Constituents of the Twelfth Congressional District, At Braintree, September 17th, 1842* (Boston: J. H. Eastburn, Printer, 1842), p. 21.

76. "In the last resort, a remedy must be obtained from the people, who can, by the election of more faithful representatives, annul the acts of the usurpers." James Madison, "The Federalist No. 44, Restrictions on the Authority of the Several States," *The Avalon Project*, January 25, 1788 (at: http://www.constitution.org/fed/federa44.htm); see also, David Franklin Houston, *A Critical Study of Nullification in South Carolina* (New York: Longman, Greens and Co., 1896), pp. 20-21.

77. Samuel Adams, *The Writings of Samuel Adams*, Harry Alonzo Cushing, editor (New York: G. P. Putnam's Sons, 1908), Vol. IV, p. 246, to Mrs. Adams on February 1, 1781.

78. George Washington, *Address of George Washington, President of the United States. . . Preparatory to His Declination* (Baltimore: George and Henry S. Keatinge, 1796), p. 22.

Appendix C:
The Declaration of Independence

Appendix C:
The Declaration of Independence

IN CONGRESS, July 4, 1776.

The unanimous Declaration of the thirteen united States of America,

When in the Course of human events, it becomes necessary for one people to dissolve the political bands which have connected them with another, and to assume among the powers of the earth, the separate and equal station to which the Laws of Nature and of Nature's God entitle them, a decent respect to the opinions of mankind requires that they should declare the causes which impel them to the separation.

We hold these truths to be self-evident, that all men are created equal, that they are endowed by their Creator with certain unalienable Rights, that among these are Life, Liberty and the pursuit of Happiness. --That to secure these rights, Governments are instituted among Men, deriving their just powers from the consent of the governed, -- That whenever any Form of Government becomes destructive of these ends, it is the Right of the People to alter or to abolish it, and to institute new Government, laying its foundation on such principles and organizing its powers in such form, as to them shall seem most likely to effect their Safety and Happiness. Prudence, indeed, will dictate that Governments long established should not be changed for light and transient causes; and accordingly all experience hath shewn, that mankind are more disposed to suffer, while evils are sufferable, than to right themselves by abolishing the forms to which they are accustomed. But when a long train of abuses and usurpations, pursuing invariably the same Object evinces a design to reduce them under absolute Despotism, it is their right, it is their duty, to throw off such Government, and to provide new Guards for their future security. Such has been the patient sufferance of these Colonies; and such is now the necessity which constrains them to alter their former Systems of Government. The history of the present

King of Great Britain is a history of repeated injuries and usurpations, all having in direct object the establishment of an absolute Tyranny over these States. To prove this, let Facts be submitted to a candid world.

He has refused his Assent to Laws, the most wholesome and necessary for the public good.

He has forbidden his Governors to pass Laws of immediate and pressing importance, unless suspended in their operation till his Assent should be obtained; and when so suspended, he has utterly neglected to attend to them.

He has refused to pass other Laws for the accommodation of large districts of people, unless those people would relinquish the right of Representation in the Legislature, a right inestimable to them and formidable to tyrants only.

He has called together legislative bodies at places unusual, uncomfortable, and distant from the depository of their public Records, for the sole purpose of fatiguing them into compliance with his measures.

He has dissolved Representative Houses repeatedly, for opposing with manly firmness his invasions on the rights of the people.

He has refused for a long time, after such dissolutions, to cause others to be elected; whereby the Legislative powers, incapable of Annihilation, have returned to the People at large for their exercise; the State remaining in the mean time exposed to all the dangers of invasion from without, and convulsions within.

He has endeavoured to prevent the population of these States; for that purpose obstructing the Laws for Naturalization of Foreigners; refusing to pass others to encourage their migrations hither, and raising the conditions of new Appropriations of Lands.

He has obstructed the Administration of Justice, by refusing his Assent to Laws for establishing Judiciary powers.

He has made Judges dependent on his Will alone, for the tenure of their offices, and the amount and payment of their salaries.

He has erected a multitude of New Offices, and sent hither swarms of Officers to harrass our people, and eat out their substance.

He has kept among us, in times of peace, Standing Armies without the Consent of our legislatures.

He has affected to render the Military independent of and superior to the Civil power.

He has combined with others to subject us to a jurisdiction foreign to our constitution, and unacknowledged by our laws; giving his Assent to their Acts of pretended Legislation:

For Quartering large bodies of armed troops among us:

For protecting them, by a mock Trial, from punishment for any Murders which they should commit on the Inhabitants of these States:

For cutting off our Trade with all parts of the world:

For imposing Taxes on us without our Consent:

For depriving us in many cases, of the benefits of Trial by Jury:

For transporting us beyond Seas to be tried for pretended offences

For abolishing the free System of English Laws in a neighbouring Province, establishing therein an Arbitrary government, and enlarging its Boundaries so as to render it at once an example and fit instrument for introducing the same absolute rule into these Colonies:

For taking away our Charters, abolishing our most valuable Laws, and altering fundamentally the Forms of our Governments:

For suspending our own Legislatures, and declaring themselves invested with power to legislate for us in all cases whatsoever.

He has abdicated Government here, by declaring us out of his Protection and waging War against us.

He has plundered our seas, ravaged our Coasts, burnt our towns, and destroyed the lives of our people.

He is at this time transporting large Armies of foreign Mercenaries to compleat the works of death, desolation and tyranny, already begun with circumstances of Cruelty & perfidy scarcely paralleled in the most barbarous ages, and totally unworthy the Head of a civilized nation.

He has constrained our fellow Citizens taken Captive on the high Seas to bear Arms against their Country, to become the executioners of their friends and Brethren, or to fall themselves by their Hands.

He has excited domestic insurrections amongst us, and has endeavoured to bring on the inhabitants of our frontiers, the merciless

Indian Savages, whose known rule of warfare, is an undistinguished destruction of all ages, sexes and conditions.

In every stage of these Oppressions We have Petitioned for Redress in the most humble terms: Our repeated Petitions have been answered only by repeated injury. A Prince whose character is thus marked by every act which may define a Tyrant, is unfit to be the ruler of a free people.

Nor have We been wanting in attentions to our Brittish brethren. We have warned them from time to time of attempts by their legislature to extend an unwarrantable jurisdiction over us. We have reminded them of the circumstances of our emigration and settlement here. We have appealed to their native justice and magnanimity, and we have conjured them by the ties of our common kindred to disavow these usurpations, which, would inevitably interrupt our connections and correspondence. They too have been deaf to the voice of justice and of consanguinity. We must, therefore, acquiesce in the necessity, which denounces our Separation, and hold them, as we hold the rest of mankind, Enemies in War, in Peace Friends.

We, therefore, the Representatives of the united States of America, in General Congress, Assembled, appealing to the Supreme Judge of the world for the rectitude of our intentions, do, in the Name, and by Authority of the good People of these Colonies, solemnly publish and declare, That these United Colonies are, and of Right ought to be Free and Independent States; that they are Absolved from all Allegiance to the British Crown, and that all political connection between them and the State of Great Britain, is and ought to be totally dissolved; and that as Free and Independent States, they have full Power to levy War, conclude Peace, contract Alliances, establish Commerce, and to do all other Acts and Things which Independent States may of right do. And for the support of this Declaration, with a firm reliance on the protection of divine Providence, we mutually pledge to each other our Lives, our Fortunes and our sacred Honor.

The 56 signatures on the Declaration:

Connecticut:
Roger Sherman
Samuel Huntington
William Williams
Oliver Wolcott

Delaware:
Caesar Rodney
George Read
Thomas McKean

Georgia:
Button Gwinnett
Lyman Hall
George Walton

Maryland:
Samuel Chase
William Paca
Thomas Stone
Charles Carroll of
Carrollton

Massachusetts:
Samuel Adams
John Adams
John Hancock
Robert Treat Paine
Elbridge Gerry

New Hampshire:
Josiah Bartlett
William Whipple
Matthew Thornton

New Jersey:
Richard Stockton
John Witherspoon
Francis Hopkinson
John Hart
Abraham Clark

New York:
William Floyd
Philip Livingston
Francis Lewis
Lewis Morris

North Carolina:
William Hooper
Joseph Hewes
John Penn

South Carolina:
Edward Rutledge
Thomas Heyward, Jr.
Thomas Lynch, Jr.
Arthur Middleton

Pennsylvania:
Robert Morris
Benjamin Rush
Benjamin Franklin
John Morton
George Clymer
James Smith
George Taylor
James Wilson
George Ross

Rhode Island:
Stephen Hopkins
William Ellery

Virginia:
George Wythe
Richard Henry Lee
Thomas Jefferson
Benjamin Harrison
Thomas Nelson, Jr.
Francis Lightfoot Lee
Carter Braxton

Appendix D:

The Second Amendment

by

David Barton

(re-printed with permission of David Barton)

The Second Amendment: Preserving the Inalienable Right of Individual Self-Protection
Copyright © 2000, David Barton
1st Edition, 6th Printing, 2017

Additional materials available from:
WallBuilders
P. O. Box 397
Aledo, TX 76008
(817) 441-6044
www.wallbuilders.com

Cover Painting:
Battle of Lexington, April 19, 1775. Oil on canvas by William Barnes Wollen (1857-1936), 1910.
Courtesy of the Director, National Army Museum, London

Cover Design:
Jeremiah Pent
Lincoln-Jackson
838 Walden Dr.
Franklin, TN 37064

ISBN 10: 0-925279-77-3
ISBN 13: 978-0-925279-77-4

Printed in the United States of America

The

Second Amendment

Preserving the Inalienable Right of
Individual Self-Protection

David Barton

Aledo, Texas
www.wallbuilders.com

Table of Contents

Blank pages 4, 64, & 78 deleted for this Appendix

The Second Amendment
Preserving the Inalienable Right of
Individual Self-Protection

The Second Amendment has become one of the most controversial parts of the Constitution. That Amendment, written in 1789 by the First Congress and ratified in 1791 by the States as part of the original Bill of Rights, states:

A well regulated militia being necessary to the security of a free state, the right of the people to keep and bear arms shall not be infringed.

The meaning of the right "to keep and bear arms," and the segment of the citizenry to which that right applies, has been heatedly and vociferously debated in recent years. Specifically, what does "people" mean? Does "people" refer to the collective body (the "militia") or does "people" refer to every citizen individually?

While gun rights supporters assert that the right to keep and bear arms is an individual right like the freedom of speech or religion, gun opponents assert that the right pertains only to collective bodies (e.g., the military, police, National Guard, etc.) and not to individuals. According to gun opponents:

> [T]here is *no* individual right to bear arms in the Bill of Rights. [1] *USA Today* (emphasis added)

> [L]aw-abiding Americans have *no* unconditional right to firearms access. [2] *New York Post* (emphasis added)

> The debate over gun control offers a revealing case study of the misuse of the Constitution. . . . [T]he idea that the Bill of Rights guarantees each individual a right to own a gun. . . . [is] a constitutional illusion. [3] *The San Francisco Barrister*

> [T]he sale, manufacture, and possession of handguns ought to be banned. . . . [W]e do not believe the 2nd Amendment guarantees an individual right to keep them. [4] *The Washington Post*

[T]here is *no* Constitutional guarantee for private ownership of firearms. [5] *Austin American Statesman* (emphasis added)

Believing that the Constitution offers no protection for individual gun ownership, gun opponents therefore encourage efforts to restrict or ban citizen access to firearms, particularly handguns. They frequently utilize highly-publicized, tragic instances of violence (such as those at Columbine, Fort Worth, Seattle, etc.) to bolster their argument that guns should be left only in the hands of "professionals." For example:

There is no reason for anyone in the country, for anyone except a police officer or a military person, to buy, to own, to have, to use, a handgun. [6] *Michael Gartner, former president of NBC News*

[T]he Second Amendment . . . protects only the right to "bear arms" for the purpose of service in the "militia," and . . . *not* . . . firearm ownership unrelated to militia service. [7] *Statement filed by fifty-two law professors and historians in a Second Amendment lawsuit* (emphasis added)

[T]he individual's right to bear arms applies only to the preservation or efficiency of a "well-regulated militia." Except for lawful police and

military purposes, the possession of weapons by individuals is *not* constitutionally protected. [8]
The ACLU (emphasis added)

One of the few things on which both gun rights supporters and gun rights opponents agree is that law enforcement officials, the militia, and the military do have the right to keep and bear arms. Therefore, this work will examine the contested scope of the Second Amendment: do individual citizens have a constitutionally-protected right "to keep and bear arms"? Four sources of information will be examined to determine the answer: (1) America's earliest legal commentaries, (2) the writings of the Founding Fathers, (3) early State laws, and (4) State constitutions.

These four categories of information will indisputably demonstrate that a citizen's right to keep and bear arms is an individually guaranteed right and that efforts to restrict or regulate gun possession by ordinary law-abiding citizens – no matter what "humanitarian" or alleged "historical" arguments might undergird such efforts – are unequivocal violations of the explicit protections and original intentions of the Constitution. In fact, after examining the historical documents and records surrounding the framing of the Second Amendment, if any individual or group still claims that the right to keep and bear arms is not an individual right, then that individual or group is just as likely – to use the words of nineteenth-century military chaplain William Biederwolf – to "look all over the sky at high noon on a cloudless day and not see the sun." [9]

I. Early Legal Commentaries

Among the many sources which indicate the original intent, and thus the proper interpretation, of the Second Amendment are early legal commentaries. Examining these commentaries (which often contain the legal writings which influenced the framing of the Second Amendment as well as the writings of those who drafted that Amendment) is vital to understanding the reasoning behind and scope of protection intended by that Amendment.

In fact, a common error in constitutional interpretation is the failure to examine a document according to its original meaning. As explained by Noah Webster (the Founder responsible for Article I, Section 8, ¶ 8 of the Constitution), not only misinterpretation but even serious error can result when original meanings are ignored:

> [I]n the lapse of two or three centuries, changes have taken place which . . . obscure the sense of the original languages. . . . The effect of these changes is that some words are . . . now used in a sense different from that

which they had ... [and thus] present a wrong signification or false ideas. Whenever words are understood in a sense different from that which they had when introduced.... mistakes may be very injurious. [10]

To avoid such "injurious mistakes," President Thomas Jefferson admonished Supreme Court Justice William Johnson:

On every question of construction, carry ourselves back to the time when the Constitution was adopted, recollect the spirit manifested in the debates, and instead of trying what meaning may be squeezed out of the text, or invented against it, conform to the probable one in which it was passed. [11]

Constitution signer James Madison agreed with this approach, stating:

I entirely concur in the propriety of resorting to the sense in which the Constitution was accepted and ratified by the nation. In that sense *alone* it is the *legitimate* Constitution. And if that be not the guide in expounding it, there can be no security for a consistent and stable, more than for a faithful, exercise of its powers.... What a metamorphosis would be produced in the code of law if all its ancient phraseology were to be taken in its modern sense. [12] (emphasis added)

James Wilson, an original Justice on the Supreme Court, similarly exhorted:

The first and governing maxim in the interpretation of a statute is to discover the meaning of those who made it. [13]

Justice Joseph Story (appointed to the Supreme Court by President James Madison) also emphasized this principle, declaring:

The first and fundamental rule in the interpretation of all [documents] is to construe them according to the sense of the terms and the intention of the parties. [14]

The following excerpts from legal commentaries written both before and after the adoption of the Constitution and its Second Amendment establish the understanding of the rights addressed by that Amendment at the time it was framed. As will be demonstrated, the Second Amendment was to protect what was frequently called "the first law of nature" – the right of self-protection. This right of self-protection was, in fact, considered an inalienable right – a right guaranteed to every citizen individually.

However, before establishing that the Second Amendment was intended to secure an individual's right "to keep and bear arms" as an inalienable right, it is important to establish just what an inalienable right is. Constitution signer John Dickinson, like many of the others in his day, defined an inalienable right as a right "which God gave to you and which no inferior power has a right to take away." [15]

Our Founders believed that it was the duty of government to protect inalienable, or God-granted, rights from encroachment or usurpation. This was made clear by James Wilson.

James Wilson was one of only six Founders who signed both the Declaration of Independence and the Constitution; he was the second most-active member of the Constitutional Convention, speaking 168 times on the floor of the Convention; he was a law professor; he was nominated by President George Washington as an original Justice to the U.S. Supreme Court; and in 1792, he was coauthor of America's first legal commentaries on the Constitution. [16] Wilson helped lay the foundation for a purely American system of jurisprudence and started the first organized system of legal training in America. [17] In fact, James Wilson conducted his legal training for students while simultaneously sitting as a Justice on the Supreme Court.

Wilson taught his students that the specific protections found in our government documents did not create new rights but rather secured old rights – that our documents were merely . . .

> . . . to acquire a new security for the possession or the recovery of those rights to . . . which we were *previously entitled* by the immediate gift or by the unerring law of our all-wise and all-beneficent Creator. [18] (emphasis added)

Wilson then asserted that . . .

> . . . every government which has not this in view as its principal object is not a government of the legitimate kind. [19]

John Adams agreed, declaring that:

> *Rights* [are] antecedent to all earthly government; *Rights* . . . cannot be repealed or restrained by human laws; *Rights* [are] derived from the great Legislator of the universe. [20]

Thomas Jefferson similarly explained that government . . .

> . . . is to declare and enforce only our *natural rights* and duties and to take *none* of them from us. [21] (emphasis added)

The Second Amendment (as well as the other Amendments) did not grant or bestow any new right on citizens; rather, it simply recognized and provided, in the words of James Wilson, "a new security" to the already existing, natural, God-given rights of citizens for their own self-defense. As Alexander Hamilton affirmed:

> [T]he Supreme Being gave existence to man, together with the *means of preserving* and beautifying that existence. He ... invested him [man] with an *inviolable right* to personal liberty and *personal safety.* [22] (emphasis added)

Since the right to self-defense was an inalienable personal right, the Second Amendment simply assured each citizen that he would have the tools necessary to defend his life, family, or property from aggression, whether from an individual or a government. That the Second Amendment simply secured in writing a right which God had already conferred on His creation was confirmed in the legal commentaries that undergirded American law. †

---

† Although much less emphasized during the framing of the Second Amendment, gun activities related to hunting were also covered under the protections of that Amendment since it was also considered to be a natural, God-given right for each individual to be able to provide food for his table through what Pennsylvania in 1787 described as "killing game." [23]

One such commentary was *Blackstone's Commentaries on the Laws*, the most influential legal commentary at the time of the framing of the Second Amendment. Originally introduced in America in 1766 while America was still a British colony, *Blackstone's* eventually became *the* standard for American attorneys and judges. In fact, Thomas Jefferson observed that American lawyers used *Blackstone's* with the same dedication and reverence that Muslims used the Koran. [24] Concerning the right of citizens to own and use arms, *Blackstone's* declared:

> The ... right of the [citizens] that I shall at present mention, is that of having arms for their defense. ... [This is] the natural right of resistance and self-preservation when the sanctions of society and laws are found insufficient to restrain the violence of oppression. ... [T]o vindicate these rights when actually violated or attacked, the [citizens] are entitled, in the first place, to the regular administration and free course of justice in the courts of law; next, to the right of petitioning the [government] for redress of grievances; and lastly, to the right of having and using arms for self-preservation and defense. [25]

Not only did the Second Amendment secure what Blackstone had called "the right of having and using arms" for "the natural right of resistance and self-preservation" but our Founders further believed that it was a *duty* for every citizen to be willing to exercise that right when necessary. This was made clear by James Wilson, who declared:

> Homicide is enjoined [required] when it is necessary for the defense of one's person or house.... [I]t is the great natural law of self-preservation which, as we have seen, cannot be repealed or superseded or suspended by any human institution. This law, however, is expressly recognized in the constitution of Pennsylvania: "The *right* of the citizens *to bear arms in the **defense of themselves** shall not be questioned.*"... [E]very man's house is deemed, by the law, to be his castle; and the law, while it invests him with the power, [places] on him the duty of the commanding officer [of his house]. "Every man's house is his castle ... and if any one be robbed in it, it shall be esteemed his own default and negligence." [26] (emphasis added)

Zephaniah Swift, author of America's first legal text in 1792, similarly confirmed:

> [S]elf-defense, or self-preservation, is one of the first laws of nature, which no man ever resigned upon entering into society. [27]

Another legal commentary addressing the fundamental rights recognized in the Second Amendment was that of St. George Tucker. Tucker, an attorney and a military officer wounded twice during the American Revolution, was one of the leaders of the 1786 Annapolis Convention that led to the convening of the Constitutional Convention in 1787. Tucker became one of the most distinguished legal scholars in early America, serving as a law professor in the College of William and Mary, a justice on the Virginia Supreme Court, and as a federal judge under President James Madison. Tucker, however, was perhaps most famous for his annotated edition of *Blackstone's Commentaries*. In that celebrated work, Tucker declared:

> The right of self defence is the first law of nature: in most governments it has been the study of rulers to confine this right within the narrowest limits possible. Wherever . . . the right of the people to keep and bear arms is, under any color or pretext whatsoever, prohibited, liberty, if not already annihilated, is on the brink of destruction. [28]

A concurring view is presented in the legal commentary authored by William Rawle. Rawle was offered (but declined) a federal judgeship by President

George Washington and instead accepted from him the position of a U.S. Attorney. Rawle later founded an early legal society that became a law academy. In 1825, he published his *View of the Constitution,* one of America's first extensive commentaries on the Constitution. That work became an early classic, serving as a textbook in numerous legal institutions as well as in the U.S. Military Academy. In his commentary, Rawle explained:

> In the Second [Amendment], it is declared. . . . that "the right of the people to keep and bear arms shall not be infringed." The prohibition is general. No clause in the Constitution could, by *any* rule of construction, be conceived to give the Congress a power to disarm the people. A flagitious [flagrantly wicked] attempt could only be made under some general pretense by a State legislature. But if, in any blind pursuit of inordinate power, either [the State or federal government] should attempt it, this Amendment may be appealed to as a restraint on both. [29] (emphasis added)

The year after Rawle released his work, an even more comprehensive legal commentary was published by Chancellor James Kent. Kent is recognized by historians and scholars as one of the two "Fathers of American Jurisprudence," sharing that honor with Supreme Court Justice Joseph Story. Kent had embarked on the practice of law after reading *Blackstone's Commentaries* during the American Revolution; and during the Constitutional Convention of 1787, he became a close friend of many of the delegates. He subsequently became a law professor and a justice on the New York Supreme Court, where he instituted the practice of handing down written opinions. In 1826, Kent issued his *Commentaries on American Law*, still considered today as a "foremost American institutional legal treatise." [30] In fact, Supreme Court Justice Lewis Powell (1907-1998) declared of Kent's commentaries that, "One who desires a brief review of the foundation stones of our constitutional jurisprudence can go nowhere else with such profit." [31] In those commentaries, Kent declared:

> The municipal law of our . . . country has likewise left with *individuals* the exercise of the natural right of self-defense. . . . The right of self-defense . . . is founded in the law of nature, and is not, and *cannot* be, superseded by the law of society. [32] (emphasis added)

Perhaps the most authoritative legal commentary ever written on the U.S. Constitution was that of

Joseph Story. Story was the son of one of the "Indians" at the Boston Tea Party; he was the founder of Harvard Law School; he was called the "foremost of American legal writers"; [33] he was nominated to the U.S. Supreme Court by President James Madison; and he is the youngest Justice ever appointed to the Court. During his 34 years on the Court, Story authored 286 opinions, of which ninety-four percent were recorded as the Court's opinion. Story was one of America's most prolific judicial writers, and – along with James Kent – is titled a "Father of American Jurisprudence." In his 1833 *Commentaries on the United States Constitution*, Justice Story declared:

> The next amendment is: "A well-regulated militia being necessary to the security of a free state, the right of the people to keep and bear arms shall not be infringed. " The importance of this article will scarcely be doubted by any persons who have duly reflected upon the subject. . . . The right of the citizens to keep and bear arms has justly been considered as the palladium of the liberties of a republic since it offers a strong moral check against the usurpation and arbitrary power of rulers; and will generally, even if these are successful in the first instance, enable the people to resist and triumph over them. . . . There is certainly

no small danger that indifference may lead to disgust, and disgust to contempt, and thus gradually undermine all the protection intended by this clause of our national Bill of Rights. [34]

(Justice Story here asserts that which will be reconfirmed in subsequent sections: that the scope of the Second Amendment allowed citizens to defend themselves not only against the aggression of other individuals but also against that of government – "against the usurpation and arbitrary power of rulers.")

Henry St. George Tucker (son of St. George Tucker mentioned earlier) was another distinguished legal scholar. Serving as a soldier in the War of 1812 and afterwards as a U.S. Congressman, he became the Chancellor of a law school and spent 17 years as a judge. In his 1844 legal lectures, Tucker reaffirmed what his legal predecessors had already declared:

[T]he law of self-preservation. . . . is indeed familiarly styled the first law of nature. . . . [It] is recognized, *sub modo,* by the laws of every civilized country. . . . The right of self-defense, (and with it of self-preservation), may, without danger of controversy, therefore be laid down as the first law of nature. Nor is it . . . lost by entering into society. [35]

Another significant legal commentary was that of John Randolph Tucker. Tucker was dean of a law school, a constitutional law professor, the Attorney General of Virginia, and the President of the American Bar Association. In 1899, Tucker authored his two-volume commentaries on the Constitution. In those commentaries, Tucker explained:

> The Second Amendment reads thus: "A well regulated militia being necessary to the security of a free State, the right of the people to keep and bear arms shall not be infringed." This prohibition indicates that the security of liberty against the tyrannical tendency of government is only to be found in the right of the people to keep and bear arms in resisting the wrongs of government. [36]

Clearly, legal commentaries and commentators across the centuries agreed: there was an inherent, natural right of self-defense and self-preservation of which the "right to keep and bear arms" was intrinsic, belonging to every individual. In fact, the Senate Judiciary Committee has even noted:

> The proposal [for the wording of the Second Amendment] finally passed the House in its present form: "A well regulated militia, being necessary to the security of a free state the right of the people to keep and bear arms, shall not be

infringed." In this form it was submitted into the Senate, which passed it the following day. The Senate in the process indicated its intent that the right be an *individual* one, for *private* purposes, by *rejecting* an amendment which would have limited the keeping and bearing of arms to bearing "for the common defense".... The conclusion is thus inescapable that the history, concept, and wording of the Second Amendment to the Constitution of the United States, as well as its interpretation by every major commentator and court in the first half-century after its ratification, indicates that what is protected is an *individual* right of a *private citizen* to own and carry fire-arms in a peaceful manner. [37]

(emphasis added)

II. Views of the Founding Fathers

Another important source for establishing the scope and protections of the Second Amendment is the declarations of those Founding Fathers under whose watchful eye both the government and the Second Amendment were created. Those Founders confirm that every citizen not only has a right to life, liberty, and property but also the natural right to use force to preserve and defend those rights. Notice some of their emphatic declarations on this subject:

> Resistance to sudden violence for the preservation not only of my person, my limbs, and life, but of my property, is an indisputable right of nature which I never surrendered to the public by the compact of society and which, perhaps, I could not surrender if I would. .... [T]he maxims of the law and the precepts of Christianity are precisely coincident in relation to this subject. [38] JOHN ADAMS, U.S. PRESIDENT, SIGNER OF THE DECLARATION, ONE OF THE TWO SIGNERS OF THE BILL OF RIGHTS

> Among the natural rights of the Colonists are these: first, a right to life; secondly, to liberty; thirdly, to property – together with the right to support and defend them in the best manner they can. [39] SAMUEL ADAMS, SIGNER OF THE DECLARATION, "FATHER OF THE AMERICAN REVOLUTION"

[T]he said Constitution [should] be never construed . . . to prevent the people of the United States, who are peaceable citizens, from keeping their own arms. [40] SAMUEL ADAMS, SIGNER OF THE DECLARATION, "FATHER OF THE AMERICAN REVOLUTION"

The right . . . of bearing arms . . . is declared to be inherent in the people. [41] FISHER AMES, A FRAMER OF THE SECOND AMENDMENT IN THE FIRST CONGRESS

The great object is that every man be armed. . . . Every one who is able may have a gun. But have we not learned by experience that, necessary as it is to have arms, . . . it is still far from being the case? [42] PATRICK HENRY, GOVERNOR, PATRIOT LEADER

Guard with jealous attention the public liberty. Suspect every one who approaches that jewel. Unfortunately, nothing will preserve it but downright force. Whenever you give up that force, you are inevitably ruined. [43] PATRICK HENRY, GOVERNOR, PATRIOT LEADER

[M]ankind must be prepared and fitted for the reception, enjoyment, and preservation of universal permanent peace before they will be blessed with it. Are they as yet fitted for it?

Certainly not. Even if it was practicable, would it be wise to disarm the good before "the wicked cease from troubling?" [Job 3:17] [44] JOHN JAY, ORIGINAL CHIEF-JUSTICE, U.S. SUPREME COURT

And what country can preserve its liberties if its rulers are not warned from time to time that this people preserve the spirit of resistance? Let them take arms. [45] THOMAS JEFFERSON, U.S. PRESIDENT, SIGNER OF THE DECLARATION

No [citizen] shall be debarred the use of arms within his own lands. [46] THOMAS JEFFERSON, U.S. PRESIDENT, SIGNER OF THE DECLARATION

The people are not to be disarmed of their weapons. They are left in full possession of them. . . . This is a principle which secures religious liberty most firmly. [47] ZECHARIAH JOHNSTON, REVOLUTIONARY SOLDIER, VIRGINIA LEGISLATOR, RATIFIER OF THE U.S. CONSTITUTION

[T]o preserve liberty, it is essential that the whole body of the people always possess arms, and be taught alike, especially when young, how to use them. [48] RICHARD HENRY LEE, SIGNER OF THE DECLARATION, A FRAMER OF THE SECOND AMENDMENT IN THE FIRST CONGRESS

[T]he advantage of being armed [is an advantage which] the Americans possess over the people of almost every other nation.... [I]n the several kingdoms of Europe ... the governments are afraid to trust the people with arms. [49] JAMES MADISON, U.S. PRESIDENT, SIGNER OF THE CONSTITUTION, A FRAMER OF THE SECOND AMENDMENT IN THE FIRST CONGRESS

Forty years ago, when the resolution of enslaving America was formed in Great-Britain, the British parliament was advised ... to disarm the people. That it was the best and most effectual way to enslave them. But that they should not do it openly; but to weaken them and let them sink gradually. [50] GEORGE MASON, DELEGATE TO THE CONSTITUTIONAL CONVENTION, "FATHER OF THE BILL OF RIGHTS"

I consider and fear the natural propensity of rulers to oppress the people. I wish only to prevent them from doing evil.... Divine providence has given to every individual the means of self-defense. [51] GEORGE MASON, DELEGATE TO THE CONSTITUTIONAL CONVENTION, "FATHER OF THE BILL OF RIGHTS"

I am thus far a Quaker [a pacifist]: I would gladly agree with all the world to lay aside the use of arms and settle matters by negotiation; but unless the whole will, the matter ends, and I take up my musket and thank Heaven

He has put it in my power. [52] THOMAS PAINE, PATRIOT, AUTHOR

[A]rms, like laws, discourage and keep the invader and the plunderer in awe, and preserve order in the world as well as property. The balance of power is the scale of peace. The same balance would be preserved were all the world destitute of arms, for all would be alike; but since some will not, others dare not lay them aside.... The history of every age and nation establishes these truths, and facts need but little arguments when they prove themselves. [53] THOMAS PAINE, PATRIOT, AUTHOR

A people who mean to continue free must be prepared to meet danger in person, not to rely upon the fallacious protection of . . . armies. [54] EDMUND RANDOLPH, DELEGATE TO THE CONSTITUTIONAL CONVENTION, SECRETARY OF STATE UNDER PRESIDENT GEORGE WASHINGTON

It [is] a chimerical idea to suppose that a country like this could ever be enslaved. How is an army for that purpose to. . . . subdue a nation of freemen who know how to prize liberty and who have arms in their hands? [55] THEODORE

SEDGWICK, REVOLUTIONARY SOLDIER, A FRAMER OF THE SECOND AMENDMENT IN THE FIRST CONGRESS

A free people ought . . . to be armed. [56] GEORGE WASHINGTON, U.S. PRESIDENT, SIGNER OF THE CONSTITUTION

[N]o man should scruple or hesitate a moment to use arms in defense. [57] GEORGE WASHINGTON, U.S. PRESIDENT, SIGNER OF THE CONSTITUTION

Before a standing army can rule, the people must be disarmed – as they are in almost every kingdom in Europe. The supreme power in America cannot enforce unjust laws by the sword because the whole body of the people are armed. [58] NOAH WEBSTER, REVOLUTIONARY SOLDIER, LEGISLATOR, RESPONSIBLE FOR ARTICLE I, SECTION 8, ¶ 8 OF THE CONSTITUTION

The declarations of those who framed our government and its Second Amendment confirm that the rights in that Amendment indeed secure the Divine right of individual citizens to use whatever force or arms may be necessary to preserve the other rights given to them by God and protected by the Constitution.

In fact, a work jointly authored in 1825 by William Sumner (a military general from Massachusetts) and Alden Partridge (a captain, a military instructor at

West Point, and the founder of Norwich University) observed that citizens's blessings of "having the choice of their leaders, the firesides, the temples of justice, the altars of religion, national independence and glory, which, under Providence, we have built up, will continue in permanent security" only so long as "people are trained to the use of arms and keep them in their hands." [59]

III. Early Legislative Acts

The views held by early Americans on the Second Amendment right "to keep and bear arms" were a reflection of the views previously established by experience and decades of tradition and finally incorporated by law into their own States. Those early laws provide the third source which affirms that the right "to keep and bear arms" pertains to every individual citizen.

Consider, for example, a 1623 Virginia law that prevented a citizen from traveling unless he was "well armed." [60] And in 1631, Virginia required:

> That men go not to work . . . without their arms. All men that are fitting to bear arms shall bring their pieces to the church, [and] upon pain of every offense . . . pay 2 lb of tobacco. [61]

In 1658, Virginia required every householder to have a functioning firearm within his house; and in

1673, the law provided that a citizen who claimed that he was too poor to purchase a firearm would have one purchased for him by the government, which would then require him to pay a reasonable price when  able to do so. [62] And a 1676 law declared that "Liberty is granted to all persons to carry their arms wheresoever they go." [63]

The New Plymouth Colony in 1632 required that "each person . . . have piece, powder, and shot; a sufficient musket or other serviceable piece. . . . [and] be at all times furnished with two pounds of powder and ten pounds of bullets." [64] In fact, so serious was this Colony about its citizens bearing arms that it established the following fines for those who were not armed:

> The fines of such as are defective in their arms:
> For such as are wholly defective: 10 shillings
>> that want a piece: 6 shillings
>> that want a sword: 2 shillings
>> that want powder: 5 shillings
>> that want bullets: 2 shillings. [65]

In 1639, the Newport Colony required that "none shall come to any public meeting without his weapon." [66]

In 1650, Connecticut ordered that its citizens "be always provided with, and have in readiness by them, half a pound of powder, two pound of serviceable bullets or shot, and two fathom of match to every matchlock, upon the penalty of five shillings a month for each person's default herein." [67]

And Georgia felt it necessary in 1770, "for the better security of the inhabitants," to require every resident "to carry firearms to places of public worship." [68]

Not only do these early laws recognize the right of every citizen to keep and bear arms, they further reveal that every private individual citizen was considered a part of the public defense. As explained by Richard Henry Lee, a signer of the Declaration and an original framer of the Second Amendment:

> [T]he militia shall always ... include, *according to the past and general usage of the* **States**, all men capable of bearing arms. [69] (emphasis added)

(Examples of State constitutions confirming this declaration will be presented shortly.)

For this reason, "militia" in the Second Amendment was understood to be every individual citizen rather than just the army or the organized military:

A militia . . . are in fact the people themselves. . . . [and] are for the most part employed at home in their private concerns. [70] RICHARD HENRY LEE, SIGNER OF THE DECLARATION, A FRAMER OF THE SECOND AMENDMENT IN THE FIRST CONGRESS

The militia . . . are . . . the people at large. [71] TENCH COXE, ATTORNEY GENERAL OF PENNSYLVANIA, ASSISTANT SECRETARY OF THE TREASURY UNDER PRESIDENT GEORGE WASHINGTON

The militia is composed of free citizens. [72] SAMUEL ADAMS, SIGNER OF THE DECLARATION, "FATHER OF THE AMERICAN REVOLUTION"

Who are the militia? They consist now of the whole people. [73] GEORGE MASON, DELEGATE TO THE CONSTITUTIONAL CONVENTION, "FATHER OF THE BILL OF RIGHTS"

It was not surprising, therefore, that when the United States Congress passed the first federal law on this subject (the Militia Act of 1792), it defined "militia of the United States" not as the Continental Army or any other organized military body but rather as including almost every adult male in the United States. Under that act, each adult was required – *by law* – to possess a firearm and a minimum supply of ammunition and military equipment, [74] and this law continued in force into the twentieth century. In fact, the *current* law still states, "The militia of the United States consists of *all* able-bodied males at least 17 [and] under 45 years of age." [75]

Significantly, numerous State constitutions adopted subsequent to the Second Amendment and the Militia Act of 1792 contain similar declarations. For example:

The militia shall consist of all able-bodied male persons.

ALABAMA, 1867; [76] 1875; [77] ARKANSAS, 1868; [78] 1874; [79] COLORADO, 1876; [80] FLORIDA, 1868; [81] 1885; [82] GEORGIA, 1868; [83] IDAHO, 1889; [84] ILLINOIS, 1818; [85] 1870; [86] INDIANA, 1851; [87] IOWA, 1846; [88] 1857; [89] KANSAS, 1855; [90] 1857; [91] 1858; [92] 1859; [93] KENTUCKY, 1850; [94] 1890; [95] LOUISIANA, 1868; [96] MAINE, 1819; [97] MARYLAND, 1864; [98] MICHIGAN, 1850; [99] MISSISSIPPI, 1868; [100] 1890; [101] MISSOURI, 1861; [102] 1865; [103] 1875; [104] MONTANA, 1889; [105] NEW YORK, 1894; [106] NORTH CAROLINA, 1868; [107] 1876; [108] NORTH DAKOTA, 1889; [109] OHIO, 1851; [110] OREGON, 1857; [111] SOUTH CAROLINA, 1868; [112] 1895; [113] SOUTH DAKOTA, 1889; [114] UTAH, 1895; [115] VIRGINIA, 1870; [116] WASHINGTON, 1889; [117] WYOMING, 1889 [118]

(Significantly, each of these States has its own State National Guard unit and its own separate laws regulating that body. The above militia provision, however, is separate from those laws and pertains not to the National Guard but rather to individual "able-bodied persons" outside that body.)

Thus, the State constitutions (both colonial and modern), the federal Constitution, early federal laws, and especially the declarations of those who framed the Second Amendment all confirm that the guarantees of the U. S. Constitution concerning the right to keep and bear arms were always understood to be inclusive of and extended to *every* "able-bodied citizen."

Furthermore, the federal Constitution was not formed in a vacuum, independent of the influence of the States. That is, it cannot reasonably be argued that the Second Amendment established a concept touching the right of citizen self-protection contrary to that which existed throughout the nation at that time. It is irrefutable that the views held by the States on this issue had significant impact on the drafting of the federal Second Amendment. In fact, simply consider how the Bill of Rights – including the Second Amendment – came into existence.

While the Constitutional Convention ended with a proposal for a new federal government, it closed on a somewhat divisive tone. During the Convention, George Mason had moved that a Bill of Rights be added to the Constitution to provide specific protection for States and individuals, [119] but others at the Convention opposed any Bill of Rights, and their position prevailed. [120] For this reason, Convention delegates such as George Mason, Elbridge Gerry, and Edmund Randolph refused to sign the new Constitution.

These delegates returned to their home States to lobby against the ratification of the Constitution until a Bill of Rights was added. As a result of their voices (and numerous others in the States who agreed with them), the ratification of the Constitution almost failed in Virginia, [121] Massachusetts, [122] New Hampshire, [123] and New York. [124] Rhode Island adamantly refused to ratify it, [125] and North Carolina refused to do so until limitations were placed upon the federal government.[126] Although the Constitution was eventually ratified, a clear message had been delivered: there was strong sentiment demanding the inclusion of a Bill of Rights. [†]

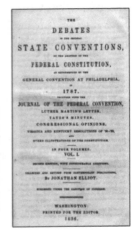

---

† The best source for examining the call for a Bill of Rights in the various State conventions is Elliot's *Debates in the Several State Conventions on the Adoption of the Federal Constitution* (1836). This is the original compilation of the records from each State's ratifying convention, and even today this work remains a primary reference, unrivaled in both scholarship and accuracy.

When the First Congress convened, Elbridge Gerry (a signer of the Declaration of Independence and one of the members of the Constitutional Convention who had refused to sign the Constitution) reminded the other Members:

> The ratification of the Constitution in several States would never have taken place had they not been assured that the[ir] objections would have been duly attended to by Congress. And I believe many members of these conventions would never have voted for it if they had not been persuaded that Congress would notice them with that candor and attention which their importance requires. [127]

Congress, therefore, did pay close attention to what the States had proposed, and did deliberate upon and create a Bill of Rights which addressed the concerns raised by the States. It is instructive to examine the suggested wording on the right to keep and bear arms which was sent to the federal government by the States who offered their suggestions for a Bill of Rights. † For example, New Hampshire's proposed wording was:

---

† Significantly, every State which submitted a proposal for a Bill of Rights included specific protection for the right to keep and bear arms. However, proposals to protect free speech and other rights appeared in only some of the proposals, thus indicating that the general consensus among the people was that the right to keep and bear arms was even more important than many other individual rights.

Congress shall never disarm any citizen. [128]

And in the Massachusetts Convention, wording had been proposed declaring:

> [T]hat the said Constitution be never construed . . . to prevent the people of the United States, who are peaceable citizens, from keeping their own arms. [129]

While New Hampshire and Massachusetts had specifically addressed only the individual right to keep and bear arms, Pennsylvania went further, proposing:

> [N]o law shall be passed for disarming the people, or any of them. [130]

An important point is made in the Pennsylvania proposal: not only did its wording make clear that the right to be armed was applicable to the collective group ("the people") but it also applied equally to every individual ("or *any* of them"). Proposals from other States confirm their desire that there should be both a collective *and* an individual right to keep and bear arms.

For example, the proposals from Virginia, New York, and Rhode Island included one clause to protect individuals, followed by a dividing semicolon, followed by a separate clause to protect the militia:

> That the people have a right to keep and bear arms; that a well-regulated militia, composed

of the body of the people trained to arms, is the proper, natural, and safe defence of a free state. [131]

It is not surprising, then, that in 1789, Albert Gallatin (one of the framers of Pennsylvania's proposals for the Bill of Rights, a U.S. Representative and Senator under President George Washington, and the Secretary of the Treasury for Presidents Jefferson and Madison) declared:

> The whole of that Bill [of Rights] is a declaration of the rights of the people at large or considered as individuals.... [I]t establishes ... rights of the *individual* as inalienable. [132] (emphasis added)

Indeed, when one examines the Bill of Rights, it is seen that *each* of the Amendments offers to every citizen a protection of his or her *individual* rights against potential abuse or intrusion by the government. † For example, the First Amendment gives individual citizens a protection of their speech and religious expression from the control of government; the Second Amendment, of their own self-defense against tyrannical individuals or governments; the Third, the sanctity of their homes against governmental military intrusion;

---

† While the federal Bill of Rights afforded to citizens protection of their individual rights from intrusive federal powers, each State's Bill of Rights had already afforded to citizens – well before the federal Bill of Rights – similar individual protections against intrusive State powers.

the Fourth, the protection of their persons and property against unreasonable searches or seizures by the government's police powers; the Fifth and Sixth, the preservation of their due-process legal rights against overly aggressive judicial powers; the Seventh, of their right to be judged by their own peers rather than by government officials; and the Eighth, their right to be protected against government tortures. The final two Amendments, the Ninth and the Tenth, simply reiterated that the government was not to encroach on any of the other individual rights retained by the people or the States. Very simply, *each* of the Amendments in the Bill of Rights afforded specific *individual* protections to every citizen.

In fact, Fisher Ames, an original framer of the Bill of Rights and of the Second Amendment in the First Congress, affirmed this view when he declared that . . .

. . . if a Bill of rights is violated, there every injured citizen may expect, and will have more complete redress, than an army of insurgents could give him. No act can have the force of law against the Bill of Rights. Every farmer ought to read it and learn its nature and value. He will prize it more than his acres; for without it, another might reap where he sows. [133]

Thomas Jefferson similarly affirmed this view when, in a letter supporting the Bill of Rights, he told James Madison:

> [A] Bill of Rights is what the people are entitled to against every government on earth, general or particular; and what no just government should refuse. [134]

James Madison acknowledged that this was indeed the sentiment behind the movement for a Bill of Rights, telling Jefferson that:

> [A]mong the advocates for the Constitution, there are some who wish for further guards to public liberty and *individual rights*. As far as these may consist of a constitutional declaration of the most essential rights, it is probable that they will be added. [135] (emphasis added)

And when the Bill of Rights was finally introduced by James Madison in the First Congress, Madison reminded the other Members:

> I believe that the great mass of the people who opposed it [the Constitution] disliked it because it did not contain effectual provisions against encroachments on particular rights. . . . But whatever may be the form which the several

States have adopted in making declarations in favor of particular rights, the great object in view is to limit and qualify the powers of government by excepting out of the grant of power those cases in which the government ought not to act. . . . [E]very government should be disarmed of powers which trench upon those particular rights. [136]

Each Amendment was to protect an individual right; and to some of those Amendments were also added a protection on collective rights (e.g., of the people to assemble, of the militia, of juries, etc.). Based, therefore, on the individual protections appearing in each Amendment, it is illogical to assert – as do gun control proponents – that the Second Amendment should be the only Amendment not to protect an individual right. Clearly, the records prove otherwise.

In fact, James Madison originally proposed that the right to keep and bear arms appear as a textual amendment to be inserted in the Constitution in Article I, Section 9 in the section limiting Congress' power over individual citizens (e.g., outlawing the suspension of habeas corpus, bills of attainder, ex post facto laws, etc.). [137] Based on his own proposal, Madison clearly viewed the right to keep and bear arms as an individual citizen's civil right.

IV. State Constitutions

Because the Second Amendment was primarily a reflection of the belief present in the individual States, the State constitutions are the fourth source that affirm that "the right to keep and bear arms" was universally understood to be an individual right. In fact, State constitutions adopted even a century-and-a-half *after* the Second Amendment still continued to reflect the original understanding. The following clauses are reflective of many others found in State constitutions on this subject:

> Through Divine goodness, *all* men have, by nature, the rights of ... enjoying and *defending* life and liberty [and] of acquiring and *protecting* reputation and property. (emphasis added)
>
> DELAWARE, 1792; [138] DELAWARE, 1831 [139]
>
> *All* men are ... endowed by their Creator with certain inalienable rights, among which are the

rights of enjoying and *defending* their lives and liberties, [and] of acquiring, possessing, and *protecting* property. (emphasis added)

SOUTH CAROLINA, 1868 [140]

All persons have certain natural, essential, and inalienable rights, among which may be reckoned the right of enjoying and *defending* their lives and liberties; [and] of acquiring, possessing, and *protecting* property. (emphasis added)

ARKANSAS, 1836; [141] 1874; [142] CALIFORNIA, 1849; [143] COLORADO, 1876; [144] FLORIDA, 1838;[145] 1868; [146] 1885; [147] IDAHO, 1889; [148] ILLINOIS, 1818; [149] INDIANA, 1816; [150] IOWA, 1820; [151] KANSAS, 1855; [152] MAINE, 1819; [153] MASSACHUSETTS, 1780; [154] NEVADA, 1864; [155] NEW HAMPSHIRE, 1783; [156] 1792; [157] 1902; [158] NEW JERSEY, 1844; [159] NORTH DAKOTA, 1889; [160] PENNSYLVANIA, 1776; [161] 1790; [162] SOUTH DAKOTA, 1889; [163] UTAH, 1895; [164] VERMONT, 1777 [165]

The right of no person to keep and bear arms in defense of his home, person and property, or in aid of the civil power when thereto legally summoned, shall be called to question.

COLORADO, 1876; [166] MISSISSIPPI, 1890; [167] MISSOURI, 1875; [168] MONTANA, 1889 [169]

The people have the right to bear arms for their security and defense.

IDAHO, 1889;[170] KANSAS, 1855;[171] UTAH, 1895 [172]

Every citizen has a right to bear arms in defense of himself and the State. (emphasis added)

ALABAMA, 1819; [173] 1865; [174] 1875; [175] 1901; [176] CONNECTICUT, 1818; [177] FLORIDA, 1868; [178] 1885; [179] INDIANA, 1816; [180] 1851; [181] MICHI-GAN, 1835; [182] 1850; [183] MISSISSIPPI, 1817; [184] 1833; [185] OHIO, 1802; [186] OREGON, 1857; [187] PENNSYLVANIA, 1776; [188] TEXAS, 1838; [189] 1845; [190] VERMONT, 1777; [191] 1793 [192]

The right of the people to keep and bear arms shall not be infringed.

GEORGIA, 1865; [193] 1877 [194]

The rights of the citizens to bear arms in defense of themselves and the State shall not be questioned.

KENTUCKY, 1799; [195] 1850; [196] MISSOURI, 1820; [197] PENNSYLVANIA, 1790; [198] SOUTH DAKOTA, 1889; [199] VERMONT, 1786; [200] 1793; [201] WASHINGTON, 1889; [202] WYOMING, 1889 [203]

V. Conclusions and Solutions

There can be no doubt that under the original intentions and interpretations, the guarantees of the Second Amendment were extended to every citizen individually. This has been demonstrated by legal commentaries, declarations of the Founding Fathers, early State laws, and State constitutions.

Nevertheless, an argument raised today against continuing those guarantees is that "times have changed"; therefore the original intentions of the Second Amendment should be modernized. Or, in the language of former Chief-Justice Earl Warren (1891-1974) in *Trop v. Dulles*, a constitutional Amendment . . .

> . . . must draw its meaning from the *evolving standards* of decency that mark the progress of a maturing society. [204] (emphasis added)

The fact that governments *do* need to change ("evolve") and to incorporate social adjustments (i.e., the ending of slavery, the granting of suffrage to women, etc.) makes the theoretical argument to "modernize" the Second Amendment appealing to many. Yet, on serious reflection, it is not reasonable to assert that an inalienable, God-given natural right has changed and thus should be "modernized," whether it be the right to life, liberty, property, etc., or the right to protect those rights. Nevertheless, for the sake of discussion, pursue the proposition that the Second Amendment should evolve.

Interestingly, two centuries ago, the drafters of the Constitution believed that times would change and therefore so should the Constitution. However, they would have vehemently disagreed with the mechanism by which this change occurs today.

The Founders made clear that when the meaning, and thus the application, of any part of the Constitution was to be altered, it was to be at the hands of the people, not at the feet of the Court or through the encroachment of a legislative body. For this reason, Article V was placed in the Constitution to establish the proper means whereby the people might adjust, or "evolve," their government:

> The Congress, whenever two thirds of both Houses shall deem it necessary, shall propose *amendments* to this Constitution, or, on the application of the legislatures of two thirds of the several States, shall call a convention for proposing amendments.

Very simply, the *people*, through the means established in our governing documents, may add amendments to the Constitution in order to modernize it as they think necessary. It is this method of updating the Constitution that *must* be followed. As Samuel Adams forcefully declared:

[T]he *people alone* have an incontestable, un-alienable, and indefeasible right to institute government and to reform, alter, or totally change the same when their protection, safety, prosperity, and happiness require it. And the federal Constitution, *according to the mode prescribed therein,* has already undergone such amendments in several parts of it as from experience has been judged necessary. [205] (emphasis added)

George Washington also warned Americans to adhere strictly to this manner of changing the meaning of the Constitution:

If, in the opinion of the people, the distribution or the modification of the constitutional powers be in any particular wrong, *let it be corrected by an **amendment** in the way which the Constitution designates.* But let there be no change by usurpation; for though this in one instance may be the instrument of good, it is the customary weapon by which free governments are destroyed. [206] (emphasis added)

Alexander Hamilton echoed this warning, declaring:

[The] Constitution is the standard to which we are to cling. Under its banners, bona fide [without deceit], we must combat our political foes, *rejecting all changes but through the channel itself provides for **amendments**.* [207] (emphasis added)

In short, if the meaning of the Second Amendment – and thus the scope of its protections – is to change, it must be done by the people themselves according to the process established in Article V. Any other method of change, whether by judicial decision, legislative action, deliberate misinterpretation, etc., is an illegitimate use and an abuse of powers and is a usurpation of the constitutionally-guaranteed rights of the people. Current efforts by judges, legislators, academia, and media crusaders to "upgrade" the meaning of the Second Amendment – despite any well-meaning intentions which might rest behind such efforts – are, as George Washington explained, "the customary weapon by which free governments are destroyed."

Furthermore, Supreme Court Justice Joseph Story explained why there can be no basis for arbitrarily evolving the transcendent, inalienable rights such as those secured by the Second Amendment. He declared:

There can be no freedom where there is no safety to property or personal rights. Whenever legislation . . . breaks in upon personal liberty or compels a surrender of personal privileges, upon any pretext, plausible or otherwise, it matters little whether it be the act of the many or the few, of the solitary despot or the assembled multitude; it is still in its essence tyranny. It matters still less what are the causes of the change; rather urged on by a spirit of innovation, or popular delusion, or State necessity (as it is falsely called), it is still power, irresponsible power, against right. [208]

Allowing any small or elite group, no matter how loud they may be or how powerful they may seem, to be the determinant in the interpretation of the Constitution places America under what President Thomas Jefferson so aptly described as "the despotism of an oligarchy." [209]

In addition to the "times change" argument for "evolving" the Second Amendment, there is also the subjective, emotional argument. That is, since every individual with any sense of humanity detests seeing families destroyed, innocent children sacrificed, and promising lives snuffed out as a result of gun violence, the argument is advanced that reducing the number of guns will produce a safer society.

While this argument appeals strongly to our humanitarian instincts, interestingly, our Founding Fathers explained why such an argument is fallacious. They – and subsequent generations of Americans – long understood that the key to a safe society rested not on the regulation of guns, swords, knives or any other kind of weapon but rather on the regulation of the heart, something accomplished only by the combined influence of religion and education.

They realized that although civil laws attempted to regulate and restrain outward conduct by defining norms of behavior, those laws could not address the heart, the actual source of violence and crime. According to Constitution signer Abraham Baldwin, this influence over the heart was "an influence beyond the reach of laws and punishments and can be claimed only by religion and education." [210]

As John Quincy Adams (a President, U.S. Representative, and U.S. Senator) similarly explained:

Human legislators can undertake only to prescribe the actions of men: they acknowledge their inability to govern and direct the sentiments of the heart. . . . It is one of the greatest marks of Divine favor . . . that [God] gave them rules . . . for the government of the heart. [211]

Thomas Jefferson similarly acknowledged:

> The precepts of philosophy . . . laid hold of ac-
> tions only. He [Jesus] pushed His scrutinies into
> the heart of man, erected His tribunal in the
> region of his thoughts, and purified the waters
> at the fountain head. [212]

Consider murder as an example. Since civil law prohibits it, how can religion contribute anything more?
Because religion, unlike civil statutes, addresses murder
before it occurs – while it is still only a thought in the
heart (see, for example, Matthew 5:22-28). Similarly,
civil law cannot prevent hate, but religion can; and
while the attitude of hate, legally speaking, is not
a crime, it often leads to a crime (assault, murder,
slander, etc.); and it is not the law, but religion, which
successfully confronts hate and thus can prevent its
crimes. Additionally, to covet is not illegal, but it, too,
often results in crimes (theft, burglary, embezzlement,
etc.); and only religion can prevent covetousness and
thus the crimes it ultimately produces. Religion ef-
fectively provides what John Quincy Adams termed
the "rules for the government of the heart" that
prevent the crimes which originate internally but
often manifest themselves externally in gun violence.

Notice how oft-repeated among our Founders was
the emphasis that this personal, internal self-gov-

ernment was a direct societal benefit resulting from the combined strength of religion and education:

[W]e have no government armed with power capable of contending with human passions unbridled by morality and religion. Avarice, ambition, revenge, or gallantry [hypocrisy] would break the strongest cords of our Constitution as a whale goes through a net. Our Constitution was made only for a moral and religious people. It is wholly inadequate to the government of any other. [213] JOHN ADAMS, U.S. PRESIDENT, SIGNER OF THE DECLARATION, ONE OF THE TWO SIGNERS OF THE BILL OF RIGHTS

[T]hree points of doctrine ... form the foundation of all morality. The first is the existence of a God; the second is the immortality of the human soul; and the third is a future state of rewards and punishments.... [Let] a man ... disbelieve either of these articles of faith and that man will have no conscience, he will have no other law than that of the tiger or the shark; the laws of man may bind him in chains or may put him to death, but they never can make him wise, virtuous, or happy. [214] JOHN QUINCY ADAMS, U.S. PRESIDENT

[N]either the wisest constitution nor the wisest laws will secure the liberty and happiness of a

people whose manners are universally corrupt. [215]
SAMUEL ADAMS, SIGNER OF THE DECLARATION,
"FATHER OF THE AMERICAN REVOLUTION"

When the minds of the people in general are viciously disposed and unprincipled, and their conduct disorderly, a free government will be attended with greater confusions and evils more horrid than the wild, uncultivated state of nature. It can only be happy when the public principles and opinions are properly directed and their manners regulated. . . . by religion and education. [216]
ABRAHAM BALDWIN, SIGNER OF THE CONSTITUTION,
A FRAMER OF THE SECOND AMENDMENT IN CONGRESS

[T]he primary objects of government are the peace, order, and prosperity of society. . . . To the promotion of these objects, particularly in a republican government, good morals are essential. Institutions for the promotion of good morals are therefore objects of legislative provision and support: and among these . . . religious institutions are eminently useful and important. [217]
OLIVER ELLSWORTH, DELEGATE TO THE CONSTI-
TUTIONAL CONVENTION, A FRAMER OF THE SECOND
AMENDMENT IN CONGRESS, CHIEF-JUSTICE OF THE
U.S. SUPREME COURT

[T]he Holy Scriptures. . . . can alone secure to society, order and peace, and to our courts of justice and constitutions of government, purity, stability, and usefulness. In vain, without the Bible, we increase penal laws and draw entrenchments around our institutions. Bibles are strong entrenchments. Where they abound, men cannot pursue wicked courses. [218] JAMES McHENRY, SIGNER OF THE CONSTITUTION, SECRETARY OF WAR UNDER PRESIDENTS GEORGE WASHINGTON AND JOHN ADAMS

Without the restraints of religion . . . men become savages. [219] BENJAMIN RUSH, SIGNER OF THE DECLARATION

Let it simply be asked, "Where is the security for property, for reputation, for life, if the sense of religious obligation desert. . . ?" [220] GEORGE WASHINGTON, U.S. PRESIDENT, SIGNER OF THE CONSTITUTION

[T]he cultivation of the religious sentiment represses licentiousness, . . . inspires respect for and order, and gives strength to the whole social fabric. [221] DANIEL WEBSTER, "DEFENDER OF THE CONSTITUTION"

[T]he education of youth should be watched with the most scrupulous attention. . . . for it is much easier to introduce and establish an effectual system for preserving morals than to correct by penal statutes the ill effects of a bad system. [222] NOAH WEBSTER, REVOLUTIONARY SOLDIER, LEGISLATOR, RESPONSIBLE FOR ARTICLE I, SECTION 8, ¶ 8 OF THE CONSTITUTION

[To] promote true religion is the best and most effectual way of making a virtuous and regular people. Love to God and love to man is the substance of religion; when these prevail, civil laws will have little to do. [223] JOHN WITHERSPOON, SIGNER OF THE DECLARATION

When religious principles are neglected, disregarded, or suppressed, government then utilizes extensive manpower and expends massive financial sums attempting to restrain behavior which is the external manifestation of internal chaos and disorder. Robert Winthrop (Speaker of the U.S. House, 1847-1849) best summarized this truth when he declared:

Men, in a word, must necessarily be controlled either by a power within them or by a power without them; either by the Word of God or by the strong arm of man; either by the Bible or by the bayonet. [224]

It is little wonder, then, that basic religious teachings were long promoted throughout society and specifically incorporated into public education. As Daniel Webster noted:

> We regard it [public education] as a wise and liberal system of police by which property, and life, and the peace of society are secured. We seek to prevent in some measure the extension of the penal code by inspiring a salutary and conservative principle of virtue and of knowledge in an early age. . . . [W]e seek . . . to turn the strong current of feeling and opinion, as well as the censures of the law and the denunciations of religion, against immorality and crime. [225]

Religious teachings were considered to be such a fundamental part of a well-rounded education that the Founders feared what might transpire if education no longer included those principles. As signer of the Declaration Benjamin Rush warned:

> In contemplating the political institutions of the United States, I lament that we waste so much time and money in punishing crimes and take so little pains to prevent them. . . . [by] the universal education of our youth in the principles . . . of the Bible. [226]

Earlier generations understood that religion – which produced morality, internal restraints, and a basic knowledge of rights and wrongs – must be publicly encouraged and supported to ensure domestic tranquility and safety. In fact, a query by Patrick Henry offered two centuries ago – a query he thought farfetched at the time – seems appropriate today:

> Are we at last brought to such an humiliating and debasing degradation [loss of morals] that we cannot be trusted with arms . . . ? [227]

Experience proves that in a nation such as ours, the promotion and encouragement of religion and morality allows government to concentrate on its primary function: serving, rather than restraining. In short, the successful key to controlling gun violence is inculcating the restraint of the heart from an early age.

Yet, in addition to learning to regulate and restrain the passions of the heart, youth were also early taught gun safety. As Richard Henry Lee, a signer of the Declaration and a framer of the Second Amendment, explained:

> [I]t is essential that the whole body of the people always possess arms and be taught alike, *especially when young*, how to use them. [228] (emphasis added)

And Thomas Jefferson similarly advised his young fifteen year-old nephew:

> A strong body makes the mind strong. As to the species of exercise, I advise the gun. While this gives a moderate exercise to the body, it gives boldness, enterprise, and independence to the mind. . . . Let your gun, therefore, be the constant companion of your walks. [229]

John Quincy Adams also believed that youth should early be instructed in the use of guns and proper gun safety. In fact, when he was dispatched by President James Madison as Minister to Russia, Adams left his three sons in the care of his younger brother, Thomas. After arriving in St. Petersburg, Adams wrote his brother with specific instructions regarding the training of the boys (George, age 9; John, age 7; and Charles, age 3) – especially George. Adams told his brother:

> One of the things which I wish to have them taught – and which no man can teach better than you – is the use and management of firearms. This must undoubtedly be done

with great caution, but it is customary among us – particularly when children are under the direction of ladies – to withhold it too much and too long from boys. The accidents which happen among children arise more frequently from their ignorance than from their misuse of weapons which they know to be dangerous. As you are a sportsman, I beg you occasionally from this time to take George out with you in your shooting excursions – teach him gradually the use of the musket, its construction, and the necessity of prudence in handling it; let him also learn the use of pistols, and exercise him at firing at a mark. [230]

Interestingly, the early years of John Quincy Adams provide a clear illustration of the training that young people received both in the governance of the heart and in the proper use of weapons. As John Quincy Adams recounted, his youthful days were during years of great stress and turmoil:

The year 1775 was the eighth year of my age. Among the first fruits of the War was the expulsion of my father's family from their peaceful abode in Boston. . . . Boston became a walled and beleaguered town. . . . For the space of twelve months, my mother with her infant children dwelt, liable every hour of the day and of the night to be butchered in cold blood or taken and carried into Boston as hostages. . . . My father was separated from his family on his way to attend the Continental Congress. And there my mother with her children lived in unintermitted danger of being consumed with them all in a conflagration kindled by a torch in the same hands which on the 17th of June lighted the fires of Charlestown. I saw with my own eyes those fires, and heard Britannia's thunders in the battle of Bunkers' Hill, and witnessed the tears of my mother and mingled with them my own at the fall of [General Joseph] Warren, a dear friend of my father and a beloved physician to me. [231]

Despite these trying circumstances, John Quincy Adams noted that his religious instruction had continued:

My mother was the daughter of a Christian clergyman, and therefore bred in the faith of deliberate detestation of war. . . . Yet, in that same spring and summer of 1775, she taught me to repeat daily, after the Lord's Prayer, before rising from bed, the *Ode of Collins* on the patriot warriors. . . . Of the impression made upon my heart by the sentiments inculcated in these beautiful effu-

sions of patriotism and poetry you may form an
estimate by the fact that now, seventy-one years
after they were thus taught me, I repeat them
from memory without reference to the book. [232]

And during that same period, the famous Massachusetts Minute Men, as they traveled to and from
the various areas of conflict, spent many a night at
the home of the Adams. On those occasions, the
eight-year-old John Quincy Adams would shoulder
his musket and perform for the Minute Men the
various musket drills that he had learned from his
father. In fact, half-a-century after the occurrence,
Adams recalled that event in a conversation with
one of those original Minute Men:

> Mr. Cary. . . . asked me if I remembered a
> company of militia who, about the time of the
> battle of Lexington in 1775, came down from
> Bridgewater and passed the night at
> my father's house and barn, at
> the foot of Penn's Hill, and
> in the midst of whom my
> father placed me, then a boy
> between seven and eight years,
> and I went through the manual
> exercise of the musket by word
> of command from one of them. I told him I

remembered it as distinctly as if it had been last week. He said he was one of that company. [233]

As he looked back on his early training in religion and weapons, John Quincy Adams remarked:

> Do you wonder that a boy of seven years of age, who witnessed this scene, should be a patriot? [234]

Training young persons both in the handling of their heart and in the handling of weapons was long proved by experience to be the best preventive for violence. In fact, so effective was this training that New York Supreme Court Justice James Kent (1763-1847, called a "Father of American Jurisprudence") once observed that violence was so rare that during a sixteen year period on the bench he had faced only eight murder cases! [235]

The successful approach to gun safety which characterized American society for generations should be reinstated today; efforts should be abandoned to encroach upon the God-given, natural, inalienable right of individuals "to keep and bear arms" secured in the Second Amendment. ■

Endnotes

1. Richard Benedetto, "Gun Rights Are A Myth," *USA Today*, December 28, 1994.

2. "Time for Gun Control," *New York Post*, August 12, 1999.

3. Dennis Henigan, "The Right To Be Armed: A Constitutional Illusion," *The San Francisco Barrister*, December, 1989.

4. "Legal Guns Kill Too," *The Washington Post*, November 5, 1999.

5. "A History of the Second Amendment," *Austin American Statesman*, April 3, 2000.

6. Michael Gartner, former president of NBC News, "Glut of Guns: What Can We Do About Them?" *USA Today*, January 16, 1992.

7. Brief for an Ad Hoc Group of [Fifty-Two] Law Professors and Historians As Amici Curiae at 3, *United States v. Timothy Joe Emerson* (5th Cir. 1999) (No. 99-10331)

8. American Civil Liberties Union (ACLU), policy statement #47, 1996.

9. *Encyclopedia of Religious Quotations*, Frank Mead, editor (New Jersey: Fleming H. Revell Company, 1965), p. 50, quoting William Biederwolf.

10. Noah Webster, *The Holy Bible . . . with Amendments of the Language* (New Haven: Durrie & Peck, 1833), p. iii.

11. Thomas Jefferson, *Memoir, Correspondence, and Miscellanies*, Thomas Jefferson Randolph, editor (Boston: Gray and Bowen, 1830), Vol. IV, p. 373, to Judge William Johnson on June 12, 1823.

12. James Madison, *Selections from the Private Correspondence of James Madison from 1813–1836*, J. C. McGuire, editor (Washington, 1853), p. 52, to Henry Lee on June 25, 1824.

13. James Wilson, *The Works of the Honorable James Wilson*, Bird Wilson, editor (Philadelphia: Bronson and Chauncey, 1804), Vol. I, p. 14, from "Lectures on Law Delivered in the College of Philadelphia; Introductory Lecture: Of the Study of the Law in the United States."

14. Joseph Story, *Commentaries on the Constitution of the United States* (Boston: Hilliard, Gray, and Company, 1833), Vol. I, p. 383, § 400.

15. John Dickinson, *Letters from a Farmer in Pennsylvania,* R. T. H. Halsey, editor (New York: The Outlook Company, 1903), p. xlii, letter to the Society of Fort St. David's, 1768; see also John Quincy Adams, *An Oration Delivered Before the Cincinnati Astronomical Society on the Occasion of Laying the Cornerstone of an Astronomical Observatory on the 10th of November, 1843* (Cincinnati: Shepard & Co., 1843), pp. 13-14.

16. James Wilson and Thomas McKean, *Commentaries on the Constitution of the United States of America* (London: J. Debrett, 1792).

17. *Dictionary of American Biography,* s.v. "Wilson, James."

18. Wilson, *Works,* Vol. II, p. 454.

19. Wilson, *Works,* Vol. II, p. 466.

20. John Adams, *The Works of John Adams,* Charles Francis Adams, editor (Boston: Charles C. Little and James Brown, 1851), Vol. III, p. 449, from his "Dissertation on the Canon and Feudal Law," 1765.

21. Jefferson, *Memoir, Correspondence, and Miscellanies,* Vol. IV, p. 278, to Francis Gilmer on June 7, 1816.

22. Alexander Hamilton, *The Farmer Refuted: Or, A More Impartial and Comprehensive View of the Dispute Between Great Britain and the Colonies* (New York: James Rivington, 1775), p. 6.

23. A report from the 1787 Pennsylvania Convention to ratify the U.S. Constitution included protection "for killing game" as part of their suggestion for the original wording of the Second Amendment (see *The Address and Reasons of Dissent of the Minority of the Convention of Pennsylvania to their Constituents* (Boston: Powers, 1787), p. 6, Art. 7; see also *The Pennsylvania Packet, and Daily Advertiser,* December 18, 1787) and this language is subsequently found in current State constitutions, including Delaware, art. 1, § 20; Nebraska, art. 1, § 1; Nevada, art. 1; New Mexico, art. II, § 6: North Dakota, art. 1, § 1; West Virginia, art. III, § 22; Wisconsin, art. 1, § 25; etc.

24. Thomas Jefferson, *Writings of Thomas Jefferson,* Albert Bergh, editor (Washington, D. C. Thomas Jefferson Memorial Association, 1904), Vol. XII, p. 392, to Governor John Tyler on May 26, 1810.

25. William Blackstone, *Commentaries on the Laws* (Philadelphia: Robert Bell, 1771), Vol. I, pp. 143-144.

26. Wilson, *Works,* Vol. III, pp. 84-85.

27. Zephaniah Swift, *A System of the Laws of the State of Connecticut* (Windham: John Byrne, 1796), Vol. II, p 302; see also Vol. II, p. 2.

28. *Blackstone's Commentaries: With Notes and Reference*, St. George Tucker, editor (Philadelphia: William Young Birch, and Abraham Small, 1803), Vol. I, p. 300.

29. William Rawle, *A View of the Constitution of the United States of America*, second edition (Philadelphia: Philip H. Nicklin, 1829), pp. 125-126.

30. *Dictionary of American Biography*, s. v. "Kent, James."

31. *Dictionary of American Biography*, s. v. "Kent, James."

32. James Kent, *Commentaries on American Law* (New York: O. Halsted, 1827), Vol. II, p. 12, "On the Absolute Rights of Persons."

33. *Dictionary of American Biography*, s. v. "Story, Joseph."

34. Story, *Commentaries*, Vol. III, pp. 746-747, § 1889 and § 1890.

35. Henry St. George Tucker, *A Few Lectures on Natural Law* (Charlottesville: James Alexander, 1844), pp. 10-11.

36. John Randolph Tucker, *The Constitution of the United States*, Henry St. George Tucker, editor (Chicago: Callaghan & Co., 1899), Vol. II, p. 671, 25;

37. *The Right to Keep and Bear Arms*, Report of the Subcommittee on the Constitution of the Committee on the Judiciary, United States Senate, Ninety-Seventh Congress, Second Session, February, 1982, pp. 9, 17.

38. John Adams, "On Private Revenge," *Boston Gazette*, September 5, 1763.

39. Samuel Adams, *The Writings of Samuel Adams*, Harry Alonzo Cushing, editor (New York: G. P. Putnam's Sons, 1906), Vol. II, p. 351, from "The Rights Of The Colonists, A List of Violations Of Rights and A Letter Of Correspondence, Adopted by the Town of Boston, November 20, 1772," *Boston Record Commissioners' Report*, Vol. XVIII, pp. 94-108.

40. *Debates and Proceedings in the Convention of the Commonwealth of Massachusetts, Held in the Year 1788* (Boston: William White, 1856), pp. 86, 266, February 6, 1788; see also William V.

Wells, *The Life and Public Service of Samuel Adams* (Boston: Little, Brown, & Co., 1865), Vol. III, p. 267.

41. Fisher Ames, *Works of Fisher Ames*, Seth Ames, editor (Boston: Little, Brown and Company, 1854), Vol. I, p. 54, to George Richards Minot on June 12, 1789.

42. *Debates and Other Proceedings of the Convention of Virginia*, David Robertson, editor (Richmond: Ritchie & Worsley and Augustine Davis, 1805), p. 275, Patrick Henry on June 14, 1788; see also *The Debates in the Several State Conventions, on the Adoption of the Federal Constitution as Recommended by the General Convention at Philadelphia in 1787*, Jonathan Elliot, editor (Washington: Printed for the Editor, 1836), Vol. III, p. 386.

43. *Debates . . . of the Convention of Virginia*, p. 43, Patrick Henry on June 5, 1788; see also Elliot's *Debates*, Vol. III, p. 45.

44. John Jay, *The Correspondence and Public Papers of John Jay*, Henry P. Johnston, editor (New York: G. P. Putnam's Sons, 1893), Vol. IV, p. 419, to John Murray, Jun., on April 15, 1818.

45. Jefferson, *Memoir, Correspondence, and Miscellanies*, Vol. II, p. 268, to Colonel Smith on November 13, 1787.

46. Thomas Jefferson, *The Works of Thomas Jefferson*, Paul L. Ford, editor (New York: G. P. Putnam's Sons, 1904), Vol. II, p. 180, from Jefferson's proposed Constitution for Virginia, June 1776.

47. *Debates . . . of the Convention of Virginia*, p. 461, Zechariah Johnson on June 25, 1788; see also Elliot's *Debates*, Vol. III, p. 646.

48. Richard Henry Lee, *An Additional Number Of Letters From The Federal Farmer To The Republican* (New York: 1788), p. 170, Letter XVIII, January 25, 1788.

49. Alexander Hamilton, John Jay, and James Madison, *The Federalist on the New Constitution* (Philadelphia: Benjamin Warner, 1818), p. 259, Federalist No. 46 by James Madison.

50. *Debates . . . of the Convention of Virginia*, p. 270, George Mason on June 14, 1788; see also Elliot's *Debates*, Vol. III, p. 380.

51. *Debates . . . of the Convention of Virginia*, p. 271, George Mason on June 14, 1788; see also Elliot's *Debates*, Vol. III, p. 381.

52. Thomas Paine, *The Writings of Thomas Paine*, Moncure Daniel Conway, editor (New York: G. P. Putnam's Sons, 1894), Vol. I, p. 55, from "Thoughts on Defensive War," *Pennsylvania Magazine*, July, 1775.

53. Paine, *Writings*, Vol. I, p. 56, from "Thoughts on Defensive War," *Pennsylvania Magazine*, July, 1775.

54. Elliot's *Debates*, Vol. IV, p. 442, Edmund Randolph in the House of Representatives on January 5, 1800.

55. *Debates . . . of Massachusetts, Held in the Year 1788*, p. 198, Theodore Sedgwick on January 24, 1788; see also Elliot's *Debates*, Vol. II, p. 97.

56. George Washington, *The Writings of George Washington*, Jared Sparks, editor (Boston: Ferdinand Andrews, 1838), Vol. XII, p. 8, from his First Annual Address to Congress on January 8, 1790.

57. George Washington, *Writings of George Washington*, John C. Fitzpatrick, editor (Washington, D. C.: U. S. Government Printing Office, 1931), Vol. II, p. 501, letter to George Mason on April 5, 1769.

58. Noah Webster, *An Examination into the Principles of the Federal Constitution Proposed by the Late Convention Held at Philadelphia* (Philadelphia: Prichard & Hall, 1787), p. 32.

59. Simon Gardner, *Observations on National Defense, Drawn from Capt. Partridge's Lecture on that Subject and from Gen. Sumner's Letter to the Venerable John Adams on the Importance of the Militia System* (Boston: Simon Gardner, 1824), p. iv.

60. *The Statutes at Large: Being A Collection of All the Laws of Virginia from the First Session of the Legislature, in the Year 1619*, William Waller Hening, editor (New York: For the editor, 1823), Vol. I, p. 127.

61. *The Statutes . . . of Virginia* (1823), Vol. I, pp. 127, 173-174, Act XLVIII and Act LI; see also Vol. II, p. 333 (1675-1676).

62. *The Right to Keep and Bear Arms*, United States Senate, p. 5; see also *The Statutes . . . of Virginia* (1823), Vol. II, pp. 304-305, Act II (1673); see also Vol. I, p. 525, Act XXV (1658-1659).

63. *The Statutes . . . of Virginia* (1823), Vol. II, p. 386.

64. *The Compact with the Charter and Laws of The Colony of New Plymouth,* William Brigham, editor (Boston: Dutton and Wentworth, 1836), pp. 44-45.

65. *The Compact . . . of New Plymouth,* p. 76.

66. *Records of the Colony of Rhode Island and Providence Plantations in New England,* J. Bartlett, editor (Providence: 1856), Vol. I, p. 94 (1639).

67. *The Code of 1650, Being a Compilation of the Earliest Laws and Orders of the General Court of Connecticut* (Hartford: Silus Andrus, 1830), p. 73.

68. *Statutes, Colonial and Revolutionary, 1768 to [1805],* Volume 19 of the Colonial Records of the State of Georgia, Allen D. Candler, editor (Atlanta: C. P. Byrd, State Printer, 1911), Vol. I, p. 137.

69. Lee, *Additional Letters,* p. 169, Letter XVIII, January 25, 1788.

70. Lee, *Additional Letters,* pp. 169-170, Letter XVIII, January 25, 1788.

71. Tench Coxe, *An Examination of the Constitution of the United States of America, Submitted to the People by the General Convention at Philadelphia, the 17th Day of September, 1787, and Since Adopted and Ratified by the Conventions of Eleven States* (Philadelphia: Zechariah Poulson, 1788), p. 21.

72. Samuel Adams, *Writings,* Vol. III, p. 251, to James Warren on January 7, 1776.

73. *Debates . . . of the Convention of Virginia,* p. 302, George Mason on June 16, 1788; see also Elliot's *Debates,* Vol. III, p. 425 (Elliot's incorrectly lists the date as June 14; it is properly June 16).

74. *An Abridgment of The Laws of The United States,* William Graydon, editor (Harrisburg: John Wyeth, 1803), p. 293, An Act of May 8, 1792.

75. *United States Code,* title 10, § 311(a).

76. Alabama Constitution (1867), art. 10, § 1.

77. Alabama Constitution (1875), art. 11, § 1.

78. Arkansas Constitution (1868), art. 11, § 1.

79. Arkansas Constitution (1874), art. 11, § 1.

80. Colorado Constitution (1876), art. 17, § 1.

81. Florida Constitution (1868), art. 12, § 1.

82. Florida Constitution (1885), art. 14, § 1.

83. Georgia Constitution (1868), art. 8, § 1.

84. Idaho Constitution (1889), art. 14, § 1.

85. Illinois Constitution (1818), art. 8, § 1.

86. Illinois Constitution (1870), art. 12, § 1.

87. Indiana Constitution (1851), art. 12, § 1.

88. Iowa Constitution (1846), art. 6, § 1.

89. Kansas Constitution (1855), art. 10, § 1.

90. Iowa Constitution (1857), art. 6, § 1.

91. Kansas Constitution (1857), art. 13, § 1.

92. Kansas Constitution (1858), art. 9, § 2.

93. Kansas Constitution (1859), art. 8, § 1

94. Kentucky Constitution (1850), art. 7, § 1.

95. Kentucky Constitution (1890), § 219.

96. Louisiana Constitution (1868), title. 8, art. 144.

97. Maine Constitution (1819), art. 7, § 5.

98. Maryland Constitution (1864), art. 9, § 1.

99. Michigan Constitution (1850), art. 17, § 1.

100. Mississippi Constitution (1868), art. 9, § 1.

101. Mississippi Constitution (1890), art. 9, § 214.

102. Missouri Constitution (1861).

103. Missouri Constitution (1865), art. 10, § 1.

104. Missouri Constitution (1875), art. 13, § 1.

105. Montana Constitution (1889), art. 14, § 1.

106. New York Constitution (1894), art. 11, § 1.

107. North Carolina Constitution (1868), art. 12, § 1.

108. North Carolina Constitution (1876), art. 12, § 1.

109. North Dakota Constitution (1889), art. 13, § 188.

110. Ohio Constitution (1851), art. 9, § 1.

111. Oregon Constitution (1857), art. 10, § 1.

112. South Carolina Constitution (1868), art. 13, § 1.

113. South Carolina Constitution (1895), art. 13, § 1.

114. South Dakota Constitution (1889), art. 15, § 1.

115. Utah Constitution (1895), art. 15, § 1.

116. Virginia Constitution (1870), art. 9, § 1.

117. Washington Constitution (1889), art. 10, § 1.

118. Wyoming Constitution (1889), art. 17, § 1.

119. James Madison, *The Papers of James Madison,* Henry D. Gilpin, editor (Washington: Langtree and O'Sullivan, 1840), Vol. III, pp. 1565-1566, September 12, 1787; see also *Records of the Federal Convention of 1787*, Max Farrand, editor (New Haven: Yale University Press, 1911), Vol. II, pp. 587-588, 637.

120. Elliot's *Debates,* Vol. I, p. 306, September 12, 1787.

121. *Debates . . . of the Convention of Virginia,* pp. 466-469, June 25, 1788; see also Elliot's *Debates,* Vol. III, pp. 652-655.

122. *Debates . . . of Massachusetts, Held in the Year 1788*, pp. 176-181, January 23, 1788; see also Elliot's *Debates,* Vol. II, pp. 87-92.

123. Joseph B. Walker, *A History of the New Hampshire Convention* (Boston: Cupples & Hurd, 1888), pp. 41-43, June 21, 1788.

124. Elliot's *Debates,* Vol. II, pp. 412-413, July 26, 1788.

125. *Collections of the Rhode Island Historical Society* (Providence: Knowles and Vose, 1843), Vol. V, pp. 320-321, March 24, 1788.

126. Elliot's *Debates,* Vol. IV, pp. 242-251, August 1-2, 1788.

127. *Annals of Congress; The Debates and Proceedings in the Congress of the United States* (Washington: Gales and Seaton, 1834), Vol. 1, p. 464, Elbridge Gerry on June 8, 1789.

128. Walker, *A History of the New Hampshire Convention,* p. 51, New Hampshire's proposals for a Bill of Rights, June 21, 1788; see also Elliot's *Debates,* Vol. I, p. 326.

129. *Debates . . . of Massachusetts, Held in the Year 1788,* p. 86, Samuel Adams, his constitutional amendment proposed during the Massachusetts ratification debates on February 6, 1788.

130. *The Address and Reasons of Dissent of the Minority of the Convention of Pennsylvania to their Constituents* (Boston: Powers, 1787), p. 6; see also *The Pennsylvania Packet, and Daily Advertiser,* December 18, 1787.

131. *Debates . . . of the Convention of Virginia*, pp. 470-473, Virginia's proposals for a Bill of Rights, June 27, 1788 (see also Elliot's *Debates,* Vol. III, p. 369); Elliot's *Debates,* Vol. I, p. 328, New York's proposals

for a Bill of Rights, July 26, 1788; and Elliot's *Debates*, Vol. I, p. 335, Rhode Island's proposals for a Bill of Rights, May 29, 1790.

132. Albert Gallatin, *The Papers of Albert Gallatin* (Philadelphia: Historic Publications, c. 1969), microform, to Alexander Addison on October 7, 1789.

133. *Independent Chronicle* (Boston), February 22, 1787, Fisher Ames writing as Camillus.

134. Jefferson, *Works* (1904), Vol. V, pp. 371-372, to James Madison on December 20, 1787.

135. James Madison, *Letters and Other Writings of James Madison, Fourth President of the United States* (New York: R. Worthington, 1884), Vol. I, p. 423, to Thomas Jefferson on October 17, 1788.

136. *Annals of Congress; The Debates and Proceedings* (1834), Vol. 1, pp. 450, 454, 458, James Madison on June 8, 1789.

137. *Annals of Congress; The Debates and Proceedings* (1834), Vol. 1, p. 451, James Madison on June 8, 1789.

138. Delaware Constitution (1792), Preamble.

139. Delaware Constitution (1831), Preamble.

140. South Carolina Constitution (1868), art. I, § 1.

141. Arkansas Constitution (1836), art. 2, § 1.

142. Arkansas Constitution (1874), art. 2, § 2.

143. California Constitution (1849), art. I, § 1.

144. Colorado Constitution (1876), art. 2, § 3.

145. Florida Constitution (1838), art. I, § 1.

146. Florida Constitution (1868), art. I, § 1.

147. Florida Constitution (1885), § 1.

148. Idaho Constitution (1889), art. I, § 1.

149. Illinois Constitution (1818), art. 8, § 1.

150. Indiana Constitution (1816), art. I, § 1.

151. Iowa Constitution (1820), art. 2, § 1.

152. Kansas Constitution (1855), art. I, § 1.

153. Maine Constitution (1819), art. I, § 1.

154. Massachusetts Constitution (1780), art. I, § 1.

155. Nevada Constitution (1864), art. I, § 1.

156. New Hampshire Constitution (1783), art. 1, § 2.

157. New Hampshire Constitution (1792), part I, art. 2.
158. New Hampshire Constitution (1902), part 1, § 2.
159. New Jersey Constitution (1844), art. I, § 1.
160. North Dakota Constitution (1889), art. I, § 1.
161. Pennsylvania Constitution (1776), art. 1.
162. Pennsylvania Constitution (1790), art. 9, § 1.
163. South Dakota Constitution (1889), art. 6, § 1.
164. Utah Constitution (1895), art. 1, § 1.
165. Vermont Constitution (1777), chapter 1, § 1.
166. Colorado Constitution (1876), art. 2, § 13.
167. Mississippi Constitution (1890), art. 3, § 12.
168. Missouri Constitution (1875), art. 1, § 17.
169. Montana Constitution (1889), art. 3, § 13.
170. Idaho Constitution (1889), art. 1, § 11.
171. Kansas Constitution (1855), art. 1, § 4.
172. Utah Constitution (1895), art. 1, § 6.
173. Alabama Constitution (1819), art. 1, § 23.
174. Alabama Constitution (1865), art. 1, § 27.
175. Alabama Constitution (1875), art. 1, § 27.
176. Alabama Constitution (1901), art. 1, § 26.
177. Connecticut Constitution (1818), art. 1, § 17.
178. Florida Constitution (1868), art. 1, § 22.
179. Florida Constitution (1885),§ 20.
180. Indiana Constitution (1816), art. 1, § 20.
181. Indiana Constitution (1851), art. 1, § 32.
182. Michigan Constitution (1835), art. 1, § 13.
183. Michigan Constitution (1850), art. 18, § 7.
184. Mississippi Constitution (1817), art. 1, § 23.
185. Mississippi Constitution (1833), art. 1, § 23.
186. Ohio Constitution (1802), § 20.
187. Oregon Constitution (1857), art. 1, § 28.
188. Pennsylvania Constitution (1776), § 13.
189. Texas Constitution (1838), § 14.
190. Texas Constitution (1845), art. 1, § 13.
191. Vermont Constitution (1777), chapter 1, § 15.

192. Vermont Constitution (1793), art. 16.

193. Georgia Constitution (1865), art. 1, § 4.

194. Georgia Constitution (1877), art. 1, § 1, part 22.

195. Kentucky Constitution (1799), § 23.

196. Kentucky Constitution (1850), § 25.

197. Missouri Constitution (1820), art. 13. § 3.

198. Pennsylvania Constitution (1790), § 21.

199. South Dakota Constitution (1889), art. 6, § 24.

200. Vermont Constitution (1786), chapter 1, § 18.

201. Vermont Constitution (1793), chapter 1, art. 16.

202. Washington Constitution (1889), art. 1 § 24.

203. Wyoming Constitution (1889), art. 1, § 24.

204. *Trop v. Dulles*, 356 U.S. 86, 101 (1958).

205. *Independent Chronicle* (Boston), January 21, 1796, Sam Adams to the legislature of Massachusetts on January 19, 1796.

206. George Washington, *Address of George Washington, President of the United States . . . Preparatory to His Declination* (Baltimore: George and Henry S. Keatinge, 1796), p. 22.

207. Alexander Hamilton, *Works* (1851), Vol. VI, p. 542, to James Bayard, April, 1802.

208. Joseph Story, *A Discourse Pronounced Upon the Inauguration of the Author, as Dane Professor of Law in Harvard University on the Twenty-Fifth Day of August, 1829* (Boston: Hilliard, Gray, Little, and Wilkins, 1829), p. 14.

209. Jefferson, *Writings* (1904), Vol. XV, p. 277, to William Charles Jarvis on September 28, 1820.

210. Charles C. Jones, *Biographical Sketches of the Delegates from Georgia to the Continental Congress* (Boston: Houghton, Mifflin and Company, 1891), p. 7.

211. John Quincy Adams, *Letters of John Quincy Adams to His Son on the Bible and its Teachings* (Auburn: James M. Alden, 1850), p. 62.

212. Jefferson, *Memoir, Correspondence, and Miscellanies* (1830), Vol. III, p. 509, from Jefferson's "Syllabus of an Estimate of the Merit of the Doctrines of Jesus Compared with Those of Others," to Dr. Benjamin Rush on April 21, 1803.

213. John Adams, *Works* (1854), Vol. IX, p. 229, to the Officers of the First Brigade of the Third Division of the Militia of Massachusetts on October 11, 1798.

214. John Quincy Adams, *Letters . . . to His Son on the Bible and its Teachings*, pp. 22-23.

215. Wells, *The Life and Public Service of Samuel Adams*, Vol. I, p. 22, quoting from a political essay by Samuel Adams published in *The Public Advertiser*, 1748.

216. Jones, *Biographical Sketches*, pp. 6-7.

217. *Connecticut Courant*, June 7, 1802, p. 3, Oliver Ellsworth, to the General Assembly of the State of Connecticut Now in Session.

218. Bernard C. Steiner, *One Hundred and Ten Years of Bible Society Work in Maryland, 1810-1920* (Baltimore: The Maryland Bible Society, 1921), p. 14.

219. Benjamin Rush, *Letters of Benjamin Rush*, L. H. Butterfield, editor (Princeton: Princeton University Press, for the American Philosophical Society, 1951), Vol. I, p. 505, "To American Farmers About to Settle in New Parts of the United States," March 1789.

220. George Washington, *Address . . . Preparatory to His Declination*, p. 23.

221. Daniel Webster, *Mr. Webster's Address at the Laying of the Cornerstone of the Addition to the Capitol, July 4, 1851* (Washington: Gideon and Co., 1851), p. 23.

222. Noah Webster, *A Collection of Essays and Fugitiv [sic] Writings on Moral, Historical, Political, and Literary Subjects* (Boston: Isaiah Thomas and E. T. Andrews, 1790), p. 22, from his "On the Education of Youth in America, 1788."

223. John Witherspoon, *The Works of John Witherspoon* (Edinburgh: J. Ogle, 1815), Vol. VII, pp. 118-119, from his Lectures on Moral Philosophy, Lecture 14, on Jurisprudence.

224. Robert Winthrop, *Addresses and Speeches on Various Occasions* (Boston: Little, Brown and Co., 1852), p. 172, from an Address Delivered at the Annual Meeting of the Massachusetts Bible Society in Boston, May 28, 1849.

THE INDIVIDUAL RIGHT OF SELF-PROTECTION 77

225. Daniel Webster, *Works of Daniel Webster* (Boston: Little, Brown and Company, 1853), Vol. I, pp. 41–42, from a speech at Plymouth on December 22, 1820.

226. Benjamin Rush, *Essays, Literary, Moral and Philosophical* (Philadelphia: Thomas and Samuel Bradford, 1798), p. 112, from his "Defense of the Use of the Bible as a School Book, March 10, 1781."

227. *Debates . . . of the Convention of Virginia,* p. 43, Patrick Henry on June 9, 1788; see also Elliot's *Debates,* Vol. III, p. 168.

228. Lee, *Additional Letters,* p. 170, Letter XVIII, January 25, 1788.

229. Jefferson, *Writings* (1903), Vol. V, p. 85, to Peter Carr on August 19, 1785.

230. John Quincy Adams, *Memoirs of John Quincy Adams, Comprising Portions of his Diary from 1795 to 1848,* Charles Francis Adams, editor (Philadelphia: J. B. Lippincott & Co., 1874), Vol. III, p. 497, to Thomas Boylston Adams, in a letter on September 8, 1810.

231. John Quincy Adams, *Memoirs,* Vol. I, p. 5, to Mr. Sturge, 1846.

232. John Quincy Adams, *Memoirs,* Vol. I, pp. 5-6, to Mr. Sturge, 1846.

233. John Quincy Adams, *Memoirs,* Vol. VII, p. 325, on August 20, 1827.

234. William H. Seward, *John Quincy Adams, Life and Public Services of John Quincy Adams, Sixth President of the United States, with The Eulogy Delivered Before the Legislature of New York* (Auburn: Derby, Miller and Company, 1849), p. 323.

235. James Kent, *Memoirs and Letters of James Kent,* William Kent, editor (Boston: Little, Brown, and Company, 1898), p. 123.

Bibliography

Books

[An] Abridgement of the Laws of the United States, or, A Complete Digest of all Such Acts of Congress as Concern the United States at Large. William Graydon, editor. Harrisburg: John Wyeth, 1803.

Adams, John. *The Works of John Adams, Second President of the United States: With a Life of the Author, Notes and Illustrations.* Charles Francis Adams, editor. Boston: Charles C. Little and James Brown, 1850-1856. Ten volumes.

Adams, John Quincy. *An Oration Delivered Before the Cincinnati Astronomical Society on the Occasion of Laying the Cornerstone of an Astronomical Observatory on the 10th of November, 1843.* Cincinnati: Shepard & Co., 1843.

Adams, John Quincy. *Letters of John Quincy Adams to His Son on the Bible and Its Teachings.* Auburn: James M. Alden, 1850.

Adams, John Quincy. *Memoirs of John Quincy Adams. Comprising Portions of His Diary from 1795 to 1848.* Charles Francis Adams, editor. Philadelphia: J. B. Lippincott and Company, 1874-1877. Twelve volumes.

Adams, Samuel. *Writings of Samuel Adams,* Harry Alonzo Cushing, editor. New York: G. P. Putnam's Sons, 1904-1908. Four volumes.

Address and Reasons of Dissent of the Minority of the Convention of Pennsylvania to their Constituents. Boston: Powers, 1787.

Ames, Fisher. *Works of Fisher Ames with a Selection from his Speeches and Correspondence.* Seth Ames editor. Boston: Little, Brown and Company, 1854. Two volumes.

Annals of Congress; Debates and Proceedings in the Congress of the United States. Washington: Gales and Seaton, 1834.

Blackstone, William. *Commentaries on the Laws of England.* Philadelphia: Robert Bell, 1769-1771. Four volumes.

Blackstone's Commentaries: With Notes and Reference, to the Constitution of the United States; and of the Commonwealth of Virginia. St. George Tucker, editor. Philadelphia: William Young Birch, and Abraham Small, 1803. Five volumes.

[The] Code of 1650, Being a Compilation of the Earliest Laws and Orders of the General Court of Connecticut. Hartford: Silus Andrus, 1830.

Collections of the Rhode Island Historical Society. Providence: Knowles and Vose, 1827-1867. Six volumes.

[The] Compact with the Charter and Laws of the Colony of New Plymouth: together with the charter of the council at Plymouth. William Brigham, editor. Boston: Dutton and Wentworth, 1836.

Coxe, Tench. *An Examination of the Constitution of the United States of America, Submitted to the People by the General Convention at Philadelphia, the 17th Day of September, 1787, and Since Adopted and Ratified by the Conventions of Eleven States.* Philadelphia: Zechariah Poulson, 1788.

Debates and Other Proceedings of the Convention of Virginia, Convened at Richmond, on Monday the Second Day of June, 1788, for the Purpose of Deliberating on the Constitution Recommended by the Grand Federal Convention. David Robertson, editor. Richmond: Ritchie & Worsley and Augustine Davis, 1805.

Debates and Proceedings in the Convention of the Commonwealth of Massachusetts, Held in the Year 1788, and which Finally Ratified the Constitution of the United States. Boston: William White, 1856.

Debates in Several State Conventions, on the Adoption of the Federal Constitution as Recommended by the General Convention at Philadelphia in 1787. Together with the Journal of the Federal Convention, Luther Martins's letter, Yates's Minutes, Congressio-

nal Opinions, Virginia and Kentucky Resolutions of '98-'99, and Other Illustrations of the Constitution. Jonathan Elliot, editor. Washington, D. C.: Printed for the Editor, 1836. Four volumes.

Dickinson, John. *Letters from a Farmer in Pennsylvania.* R. T. H. Halsey, editor. New York: The Outlook Company. 1903.

Encyclopedia of Religious Quotations. Frank Mead, editor. New Jersey: Fleming H. Revell Company, 1965.

Gallatin, Albert. *Papers of Albert Gallatin.* Philadelphia: Historic Publications, c. 1969. Microform.

Gardner, Simon. *Observations on National Defense Drawn from Capt. Partridge's Lecture on that Subject and from Gen. Sumner's Letter to the Venerable John Adams on the Importance of the Militia System.* Boston: Simon Gardner, 1824.

Hamilton, Alexander. *The Farmer Refuted: Or, A More Impartial and Comprehensive View of the Dispute Between Great Britain and the Colonies.* New York: James Rivington, 1775.

Hamilton, Alexander, John Jay, and James Madison. *The Federalist on the New Constitution;* written in 1788. Philadelphia: Benjamin Warner, 1818.

Jay, John. *Correspondence and Public Papers of John Jay First Chief-Justice of the United States, Member and President of the Continental Congress, Minister to Spain, Member of Commission to Negotiate Treaty of Independence, Envoy to Great Britain, Governor of New York, etc. 1794-1826.* Henry P. Johnston, editor. New York: G. P. Putnam's Sons, 1890-1893. Four volumes.

Jefferson, Thomas. *Memoir, Correspondence, and Miscellanies from the Papers of Thomas Jefferson.* Thomas Jefferson Randolph, editor. Boston: Gray and Bowen, 1830. Four volumes.

Jefferson, Thomas. *Works of Thomas Jefferson.* Paul L. Ford, editor. New York: G. P. Putnam's Sons, 1904-1905. Twelve volumes.

Jefferson, Thomas. *Writings of Thomas Jefferson.* Albert Bergh, editor. Washington, D.C.: Thomas Jefferson Memorial Association, 1903-1904. Twenty volumes.

Jones, Charles C. *Biographical Sketches of the Delegates from Georgia to the Continental Congress*. Boston: Houghton, Mifflin and Company, 1891.

Kent, James. *Commentaries on American Law*. New York: O. Halsted, 1826-1830. Four volumes.

Kent, James. *Memoirs and Letters of James Kent, LL. D. Late Chancellor of the State of New York. Author of "Commentaries on American Law,"* etc. William Kent, editor. Boston: Little, Brown and Company, 1898.

Lee, Richard Henry. *An Additional Number of Letters From the Federal Farmer to the Republican Leading to a Fair Examination of the System of Government Proposed by the Late Convention; to Several Essential and Necessary Alterations in it; and Calculated to Illustrate and Support the Principles and Positions Laid Down in the Preceding Letters [together with] Observations on the New Constitution, and on the Federal and State Conventions by a Columbian Patriot*. New York: 1788.

Madison, James. *Letters and Other Writings of James Madison, Fourth President of the United States*. New York: R. Worthington, 1884. Four volumes.

Madison, James. *Papers of James Madison Purchased by Order of Congress; Being His Correspondence and Reports of Debates During the Congress of The Confederation and the Reports of Debates in the Federal Convention*. Henry D. Gilpin, editor. Washington: Langtree and O'Sullivan, 1840. Three volumes.

Madison, James. *Selections from the Private Correspondence of James Madison from 1813-1836*. J. C. McGuire, editor. Washington, 1853.

Paine, Thomas. *Writings of Thomas Paine*. Moncure Daniel Conway, editor. New York: G. P. Putnam's Sons, 1894-1896. Twelve volumes.

Rawle, William. *A View of the Constitution of the United States of America*. Philadelphia: Philip H. Nicklin, 1829.

BIBLIOGRAPHY   83

Records of the Colony of Rhode Island and Providence Plantations in New England. J. Bartlett, editor. Providence: 1856-1865. Ten volumes.

Records of the Federal Convention of 1787. Max Farrand, editor. New Haven: Yale University Press, 1911. Three volumes.

Rush, Benjamin. *Essays, Literary, Moral and Philosophical.* Philadelphia: Thomas and Samuel F. Bradford, 1798.

Rush, Benjamin. *Letters of Benjamin Rush.* L. H. Butterfield, editor. Princeton: Princeton University Press for the American Philosophical Society, 1951. Two volumes.

Seward, William H. *Life and Public Services of John Quincy Adams, Sixth President of the United States, with the Eulogy Delivered Before the Legislature of New York.* Auburn: Derby, Miller and Company, 1849.

Statutes at Large: Being A Collection of All the Laws of Virginia from the First Session of the Legislature, in the Year 1619. William Waller Hening, editor. New York: Printed for the Editor, 1823. Thirteen volumes.

Statutes, Colonial and Revolutionary, 1768 to [1805]. Volume 19 of the Colonial Records of the State of Georgia. Atlanta: C. P. Byrd, State Printer, 1911. Two volumes.

Steiner, Bernard C. *One Hundred and Ten Years of Bible Society Work in Maryland, 1810-1920.* Baltimore: The Maryland Bible Society, 1921.

Story, Joseph. *Commentaries on the Constitution of the United States; with a Preliminary Review of the Constitutional History of the Colonies and States, before the Adoption of the Constitution.* Boston: Hilliard, Gray and Company, 1833. Three volumes.

Story, Joseph. *Discourse Pronounced Upon the Inauguration of the Author, as Dane Professor of Law in Harvard University on the Twenty-fifth Day of August, 1829.* Boston: Hilliard, Gray, Little, and Wilkins, 1829.

Swift, Zephaniah. *A System of the Laws of the State of Connecticut.* Windham: John Byrne, 1795-1796. Two volumes.

Tucker, Henry St. George. *A Few Lectures on Natural Law.* Charlottesville: James Alexander, 1844.

Tucker, John Randolph. *Constitution of the United States. A Critical Discussion of its Genesis, Development, and Interpretation.* Henry St. George Tucker, ed. Chicago: Callaghan & Co., 1899. 2 vol.

Walker, Joseph B. *A History of the New Hampshire Convention for the Investigation, Discussion, and Decision of the Federal Constitution: and of the Old North Meeting-House of Concord, in which it was Ratified by the Ninth State, and thus Rendered Operative, at One O'clock P.M., on Saturday, the 21st Day of June, 1788.* Boston: Cupples & Hurd, 1888.

Washington, George. *Address of George Washington, President of the United States, and Late Commander in Chief of the American Army, to the People of the United States, Preparatory to His Declination.* Baltimore: George and Henry S. Keatinge, 1796.

Washington, George. *Writings of George Washington; being his Correspondence, Addresses, Messages, and other Papers, Official and Private, Selected and Published from the Original Manuscripts with a Life of the Author, Notes and Illustrations.* Jared Sparks, editor. Boston: Ferdinand Andrews, 1834-1838. Twelve volumes.

Washington, George. *Writings of Washington.* John C. Fitzpatrick, editor. Washington, D. C.: U.S. Government Printing Office, 1931-1944. Thirty-nine volumes.

Webster, Daniel. *Mr. Webster's Address at the Laying of the Cornerstone of the Addition to the Capitol, July 4, 1851.* Washington: Gideon and Co., 1851.

Webster, Daniel. *Works of Daniel Webster.* Boston: Little, Brown and Company, 1853. Six volumes.

Webster, Noah. *A Collection of Essays and Fugitiv [sic] Writings on Moral, Historical, Political, and Literary Subjects.* Boston: Isaiah Thomas and E. T. Andrews, 1790.

BIBLIOGRAPHY   85

Webster, Noah. *An Examination into the Principles of the Federal Constitution Proposed by the Late Convention Held at Philadelphia. With Answers to the Principle Objections that have been Raised Against the System.* Philadelphia: Prichard & Hall, 1787.

Webster, Noah. *The Holy Bible, Containing the Old and New Testaments, in the Common Version. With Amendments of the Language.* New Haven: Durrie & Peck, 1833.

Wells, William V. *Life and Public Services of Samuel Adams, Being A Narrative of his Acts and Opinions, and of his Agency in Producing and Forwarding the American Revolution.* Boston: Little, Brown & Co., 1865. Three volumes.

Wilson, James. *The Works of the Honorable James Wilson, L.L.D. Late One of the Associate Justices of the Supreme Court of the United States and Professor of Law in the College of Philadelphia.* Bird Wilson, editor. Philadelphia: Bronson and Chauncey, 1804. Three volumes.

Wilson, James, Thomas McKean. *Commentaries on the Constitution of the United States of America, with that Constitution Prefixed, in which are Unfolded the Principles of Free Government and the Superior Advantages of Republicanism Demonstrated.* London: J. Debrett, 1792.

Winthrop, Robert. *Addresses and Speeches on Various Occasions.* Boston: Little, Brown and Co., 1852.

Witherspoon, John. *The Works of John Witherspoon, D. D. Sometime Minister of the Gospel at Paisley, and Late President of Princeton College, in New Jersey. Containing Essays, Sermons, &c. on Important Subjects Intended to Illustrate and Establish the Doctrine of Salvation by Grace, and to Point Out its Influence on Holiness of Life. Together with his Lectures on Moral Philosophy, Eloquence and Divinity; His Speeches in the American Congress, and Many Other Valuable Pieces, Never Before Published in this Country.* Edinburgh: J. Ogle, 1815. Ten volumes.

Articles

Adams, John. "On Private Revenge," *Boston Gazette*, September 5, 1763.

Benedetto, Richard. "Gun Rights Are A Myth," *USA Today*, December 28, 1994.

Gartner, Michael, former president of NBC News. USA Today, January 16, 1992.

Henigan, Dennis. "The Right To Be Armed: A Constitutional Illusion," *The San Francisco Barrister*, December, 1989.

"A History of the Second Amendment," *Austin American Statesman*, April 3, 2000.

"Legal Guns Kill Too," *The Washington Post*, November 5, 1999.

Paine, Thomas. "Thoughts on Defensive War," *Pennsylvania Magazine*, July, 1775.

"Time for Gun Control," *New York Post*, August 12, 1999.

Documents/Legal References

ACLU. Policy Statement #47, 1996.

Brief for an Ad Hoc Group of [Fifty-Two] Law Professors and Historians as Amici Curiae, *United States v. Timothy Joe Emerson* (5th Cir. 1999) (No. 99-10331).

Trop v. Dulles, Secretary of State, et al. 356 U.S. 86 (1958).

United States Senate, Subcommittee on the Constitution of the Committee of the Judiciary. *The Right to Keep and Bear Arms.* Ninety-Seventh Congress, Second Session, February, 1982.

Periodicals

Connecticut Courant, June 7, 1802.

Independent Chronicle (Boston), February 22, 1787.

Independent Chronicle (Boston), January 21, 1796.

[The] Pennsylvania Packet and Daily Advertiser, December 18, 1787.

Appendix E:

Endnotes & Answer Key

Appendix E: ANSWER KEY

Episode ONE

1 earn
2 first law
3 responsibility
4 roots
5 intellectual ammunition
6 militia
7 we the people
8 first law books
9 American Jurisprudence
10 individual right
11 James Wilson
12 YOU (write YOUR name in this blank!)

Episode TWO

1 formula
2 frequent recurrence
3 August 2, 1776
4 death warrant
5 Nathan Hale
6 *increased devotion*
7 Celebrate Freedom Week
8 *knowing, perceive, defend, assert*
9 quick start guide
10 identify, protect, preserve
11 original intent
12 principle
13 amended
14 original text
15 everyone
16 platform
17 application of the principles
18 separate
19 articles of incorporation

Episode TWO (continued)

20 by-laws
21 *never*
22 Richard Henry Lee
23 Benjamin Franklin, John Adams, Roger Sherman and Robert Livingston
24 Delaware, Pennsylvania, South Carolina
25 Caesar Rodney
26 Self-evident Truths
27 Endowed by Our Creator
28 Consent of the Governed
29 The Pursuit of Happiness
30 liberty WITH God
31 liberty withOUT God
32 God to the King to the people
33 God
34 the people
35 government
36 give
37 take
38 basis of liberty
39 Benjamin
40 confusion and discontent
41 private property & free enterprise
42 ourselves
43 giving or refusing
44 wise decisions
45 4
46 2
47 8
48 1
49 Sec 8, Cl 12
50 Art 1, Sec 8, Cl 14
51 3rd Amendment
52 6th & 7th Amendments

Episode THREE

1 Independence Hall
2 55
3 39
4 Benjamin Franklin and Benjamin Rush
5 Abraham Lincoln
6 Congress
7 September 25, 1789
8 New York
9 Philadelphia
10 Washington
11 twelve
12 ten
13 one
14 Liberty Bell
15 Graff
16 Thomas Jefferson
17 legislative
18 two
19 judicial
20 individual welfare
21 Original Intent
22 Congress
23 President
24 Courts
25 States; Republic
26 Amendment Process
27 Debts, Supremacy, oath, no religious test
28 Ratification & Attestation
29 Bill of Rights
30 President (EC, dates, 2 terms, DC, incapacitation)
31 Judiciary (suits against states)
32 Congress (Sen elections, terms, pay raises)
33 End slavery & establish civil rights
34 Voting Rights (race, gender, $$$, age)
35 Income Tax
36 To drink or not to drink!

Episode THREE (continued)

37 religion; speech; press; assembly; petition
38 right to bear arms
39 quartering of soldiers
40 searches & seizures
41 grand jury; double jeopardy; self-incrimination; due process; private property takings
42 speedy public jury trial; witnesses; attorney
43 civil jury trial & common law
44 excessive fines & bail; cruel & unusual punishment
45 individual rights NOT enumerated
46 federal powers limited/enumerated; rest left to states/people
47 22nd
48 Franklin Delano Roosevelt
49 state
50 state
51 vote for president
52 17th
53 U.S. Senators
54 2nd
55 Greg Watson
56 applies
57 minority
58 participate
59 18th
60 people
61 states
62 House of Representatives

Episode FOUR

1 limited government
2 "How many people live here?"
3 federal government
4 federal government
5 states
6 to itself
7 debts

Episode FOUR (continued)

8   defense
9   welfare
10 theft
11 general
12 local
13 one
14 regular
15 foreign
16 states
17 Indian tribes
18 micro-manage
19 individual enterprise
20 distrust of power
21 levels of government
22 spirit
23 patent, copyright, trademark
24 quality
25 price
26 quality
27 price
28 price or quality
29 price and quality
30 limited jurisdiction
31 government's role
32 embryonic stem cell
33 declare war
34 1784
35 mercenaries
36 foregoing

Episode FIVE

1   president
2   people
3   states
4   popular vote
5   sufficient vote

Episode FIVE (continued)

6   distribution
7   big cities
8   pure democracy
9   three
10 four
11 in TV & movies
12 Ronald Reagan
13 George W. Bush (43)
14 at least once
15 months
16 emergency situation
17 law
18 adjourn
19 Washington
20 Congress
21 passed
22 lack of accountability
23 lifetime appointments
24 Alexander Hamilton, John Jay, & James Madison
25 Legislative
26 closest to the people
27 Judiciary
28 two branches
29 responsibility
30 Congress
31 agenda
32 good behavior
33 try
34 contradicting
35 rudeness
36 high-handedness
37 bridle
38 majority
39 equal
40 each branch
41 legislature

Episode SIX

1   religion; speech; press; assembly; petition
2   nowhere
3   journal
4   One, Five
5   none
6   Thomas Jefferson
7   infringe
8   single national denomination
9   the U.S. Capitol
10 Gouverneur Morris
11 James Wilson
12 quartering of soldiers
13 prescribed by law
14 searches and seizures
15 military
16 regulations
17 compensation
18 speedy public jury trial
19 attorney
20 $20
21 jury nullification
22 bail
23 fines
24 cruel & unusual
25 enumerated
26 other parts
27 Declaration
28 end slavery
29 boundaries

Episode SEVEN

1   Five
2   two-thirds
3   three-fourths (38)
4   two-thirds (34)
5   three-fourths (38)

Episode SEVEN (continued)

6 Constitution
7 state law
8 system
9 politicians
10 check out or give up
11 use violence or intimidation
12 state nullification
13 Alien and Sedition
14 proper authority
15 undermines
16 dangerous, anarchy
17 minority
18 majority
19 reverse course
20 courts
21 unconstitutional
22 George Washington
23 Vote
24 chosen
25 20
26 36
27 537
28 leaders
29 principles
30 candidates
31 actions
32 politician
33 patriot
34 Senators
35 state
36 support
37 republic
38 amendment

APPENDIX D: ENDNOTES

i   Walker, *A History of the New Hampshire Convention*, p. 51, New Hampshire's proposals for a Bill of Rights, June 21, 1788; see also Elliot's *Debates,* Vol. I, p. 326.

ii *Debates . . . of Massachusetts, Held in the Year 1788*, p. 86, Samuel Adams, his constitutional amendment proposed during the Massachusetts ratification debates on February 6, 1788.

iii John Adams, "On Private Revenge," *Boston Gazette,* September 5, 1763.

iv "Supreme Court Justice Clarence Thomas' Wriston Lecture to the Manhattan Institute," The Wall Street Journal, 20 October 2008, p. A19

v   Abraham Lincoln, Draft of the Gettysburg Address: Nicolay Copy, November 1863; Series 3, General Correspondence, 1837-1897; The Abraham Lincoln Papers at the Library of Congress, Manuscript Division (Washington, D. C.: American Memory Project, [2000-02])

vi John Jay, The *Correspondence and Public Papers of John, Jay,* Henry P. Johnston, editor (New York: G. P. Putnam's Sons, 1890), Vol. I, pp. 163–164, from his "Charge to the Grand Jury of Ulster County" on September 9, 1777.

vii Thomas Jefferson, *Memoir, Correspondence, and Miscellanies, From the Papers of Thomas Jefferson*, Thomas Jefferson Randolph, editor (Boston: Gray and Bowen, 1830), Vol. IV, p. 373, to Judge William Johnson on June 12, 1823.

viii Joseph Story, *Commentaries on the Constitution of the United States* (Boston: Hilliard, Gray, and Company, 1833), Vol. I, p. 383, § 400.

ix John Quincy Adams, The Jubilee of the Constitution (New York: Samuel Colman, 1839), p. 54.

x   Samuel Adams, The Writing of Samuel Adams, at 357 of Volume IV (Collected & edited by Harry Alonzo Cushing, G.P. Putnam's Sons 1908).

xi Gulf, c. & s. F. R. Co. V. Ellis, 165 U.S. 150 (1897)

xii Lossing, B. J. (1870). *Lives of the signers of the Declaration of American independence. The declaration historically considered* (252). Philadelphia: Evans, Stoddart & co.

xiii Ibid., p. 254

xiv The Declaration of Independence, para. 2 (U.S. 1776).

xv   *George Washington, Address of George Washington, President of the United States
        ... Preparatory to His Declination* 22–23 (Baltimore: George and Henry S.
        Keatinge, 1796).[xv]

xvi   Thomas Jefferson, *Notes on the State of Virginia* (Philadelphia: Matthew
        Carey, 1794), Query XVIII, p. 237.[xvi]

xvii   James Madison, *Notes of Debates in the Federal Convention of 1787*, at 209-10
        (reprinted NY: W.W. Norton & Co., 1987) (1787).

xviii   Alexander Hamilton, John Jay, & James Madison, *The Federalist*
        (Philadelphia: Benjamin Warner, 1818), p. 194, James Madison,
        Federalist #38; see also Federalist #2 (p. 12) and Federalist #20 (p. 105)
        for other acknowledgments of the blessings of Providence upon
        America.

xix   Hamilton, Alexander. 1787. Christine F. Hart, *One Nation Under God*
        (NJ: American Tract Society, reprinted by Gospel Tract Society, Inc.), p.
        2. D.P. Diffine, Ph.D., *One Nation Under God—How Close a Separation?*
        (Searcy, Arkansas: Harding University, Belden Center for Private
        Enterprise Education, 6th edition, 1992), p. 9.

xx   Letters To The Marquis De Lafayette, February 7 & May28, 1788.

xxi   Thomas Jefferson, *The Jeffersonian Cyclopedia* (Funk & Wagnalls company,
        1900), page 326

xxii   Bradford's History of Plymouth Plantation, 1606-1646. Ed. William T.
        Davis. New York: Charles Scribner's Sons, 1908

xxiii   Ibid

xxiv   John M. Taylor, *Garfield of Ohio: The Available Man* (New York: W. W.
        Norton and Company, Inc.), p. 180. Quoted from "A Century of
        Progress," by James A. Garfield, published in Atlantic, July 1877.[xxiv]

xxv   Madison's Notes to the Debates in the Federal Convention of 1787, 14 August
        1787. John Francis Mercer was a Maryland Delegate to the Convention.

xxvi   James Madison letter to Andrew Stevenson; 27 Nov. 1830

xxvii   John Adams, *Works,* Vol. VI, p. 484, to John Taylor on April 15, 1814.

xxviii Benjamin Rush, *The Letters of Benjamin Rush*, L. H. Butterfield, editor
        (Princeton: Princeton University Press for the American Philosophical
        Society, 1951), Vol. I, p. 523, to John Adams on July 21, 1789.

xxix   Ex Parte Mccardle, 74 U.S. 506 (Wall.) (1868)

xxx   Jefferson, *Memoir,* Vol. IV, p. 27, to Abigail Adams on September 11, 1804.

xxxi   Thomas Jefferson, *Memoir, Correspondence, and Miscellanies, From the Papers
        of Thomas Jefferson,* Thomas Jefferson Randolph, editor (Boston: Gray

and Bowen, 1830), Vol. IV, p. 317, to Judge Spencer Roane on
September 6, 1819.

xxxii   *Debates and Proceedings,* Vol. I, p. 568, James Madison on June 18, 1789.

xxxiii U.S. Const. Amend. I.

xxxiv   U.S. Const. Art. I, § 5, cl. 3.

xxxv   William Parker Cutler and Julia Perkins Cutler, *Life, Journal, and
        Correspondence of Rev. Manasseh Cutler* (Cincinnati: Colin Robert Clarke &
        Co., 1888), Vol. II, p. 66, 119, letter to Joseph Torrey, January 4, 1802.
        Cutler meant that Jefferson attended church on January 3, 1802, for the
        first time as President. Bishop Claggett's letter of February 18, 1801,
        already revealed that as Vice-President, Jefferson went to church
        services in the House.

xxxvi   Jared Sparks, *The Life of Governeur Morris* (Boston: Gray and Bowen,
        1832), Vol. III, p. 483, from his "Notes on the Form of a Constitution
        for France."

xxxvii James Wilson, *The Works of the Honourable James Wilson,* Bird Wilson,
        editor (Philadelphia: Bronson and Chauncey, 1804), Vol. I, pp. 104–106,
        "Of the General Principles of Law and Obligation."

xxxviii *Washington's farewell address..* New York, New York Public Library, 1935.
        pg. 105; 136. Courtesy of the Milstein Division of United States History,
        Local History & Genealogy, The New York Public Library, Astor,
        Lenox and Tilden Foundations

xxxix   Noah Webster, *The History of the United States* (New Haven: Durrie and
        Peck, 1832), pp. 336–337, ¶49.

xl   Matthias Burnett, *An Election Sermon, Preached at Hartford, on the Day of the
        Anniversary Election,* May 12, 1803, at 26-27 (Hartford: Hudson &
        Goodwin, 1803).

Appendix F:
THE CONSTITUTION MADE EASY
By Michael Holler

The following is included with the permission of Michael Holler

The
CONSTITUTION
MADE *Easy*

THE UNITED STATES CONSTITUTION

Compared Side by Side with

THE UNITED STATES CONSTITUTION

In Modern English

ISBN 978-1-60725-330-3

Published in the United States by
The Friends of Freedom, Inc.
PO Box 7333, Woodland Park, CO 80863

Manufactured in the United States of America

GUIDE TO UNDERSTANDING
AND ENJOYING
THE CONSTITUTION MADE EASY

For most people, reading the *United States Constitution* is difficult, and no wonder! It was written in "legalese," and most of it is more than 200 years old. But now *The Constitution Made Easy* not only offers a modernized version for easier reading; it actually makes the meaning of the original seem to jump off the page!

Great effort was made to preserve the original meaning and intent of the Founding Fathers in this modern English version; but by keeping the original side-by-side for comparison, *The Constitution Made Easy* becomes a reference you can trust. The *Constitution* and all of the *Amendments* in this volume were carefully copied from the version maintained by the United States Government at the National Archives. The reader is invited to visit the Archives at: www.archives.gov/exhibits.

Here are a few facts and some unique features of *The Constitution Made Easy* that will make your reading more enjoyable, and avoid unnecessary confusion.

The original Constitution will *always* be on the left-hand page, and the modern English version will *always* be on the right. The two versions look very different from each other, and the headers at the top of the page confirm which version is below it.

Now, here are a few facts about the *original*. The body of the Constitution has seven large divisions called *Articles*. Each Article discusses a new subject, such as Congress, the President or the Supreme Court. The divisions within Articles are called *Sections*, and the divisions within Sections are called *Clauses*. Any given *Clause* is normally referred to by its location, such as Article I, Section VIII, Clause VII. (This particular *Clause* concerns the Post Office.) Roman numerals are used in the original.

A modern numbering plan was adopted in the modern version, so that same Clause would be referred to as Article 1, Section 8, Clause 7. A *shorthand* way of referring to it would be simply **1.8.7** (one-dot-eight-dot-seven). At the end of the Articles are the signatures of the State delegates. When the Constitution was first approved (ratified) this is all there was.

Then there are 27 *Amendments* that come after these first seven Articles. An Amendment is sometimes referred to as an *Article of Amendment.* So like other *Articles*, it may be divided into *Sections*, and several of them have been. In the modern version, one of these *Sections* (Amendment 20, Section 3) has even been divided into two *Clauses*.

Until now, one of the great barriers to understanding the Constitution was that an Amendment sometimes modified just a few words, and sometimes it completely replaced (or *superceded*) one or more full Clauses. In the National Archives version, the language that has been replaced or modified is underlined, and then the Amendment that affected it is [cited in brackets like this].

Without a modern version, readers may find themselves jumping forward to find the Amendment, then jumping back to the original, and trying to mentally *integrate* the effects of the changes. In some cases, this can be so frustrating that even a good reader may decide to put the Constitution down "for now anyway" (and sometimes does not return to it).

Now, *The Constitution Made Easy* does this work for you. All of the effects of the Amendments are included *right in the text*. If the effect was modest, only the affected words or phrases will be added or replaced. If the effect was substantial (as you will see in Article 2, Section 1), then whole Amendments may be included in the modern version to bring the content current. These Amendments are often much longer than the language they replace.

In these instances there will be more Clauses in the modern version than in the original, and so the numbering will be different. This also creates "gaps," or blank lines, in a few places in the original. To keep it clear, the original will have [bracketed information] referring to the Amendment that replaced the original wording, and the modern version will likewise refer to it, [either in brackets] or a footnote. There should never be any real need to flash back and forth between the original and the Amendments in order to understand the current meaning.

The Constitution Made Easy

It is easy to tell where paragraphs in the original begin and end, even if there is "white space" in the middle. If any line is indented, this indicates a new paragraph in the original. If it begins at the left margin, it is a continuation of the paragraph above it.

The full texts of all of the Amendments are still included after the "amended" body of the Constitution, so some of the language will be seen for a second time. This will be especially noticeable in the 12th, 20th and 25th Amendments which greatly affected Article 2, Section 1. Also noteworthy is Amendment 17 which affected the election of Senators (Article 1, Section 3).

One more note about the *shorthand* numbering plan. To make it more apparent whether the numbers refer to the body of the Constitution, or to an Amendment, the letter "C" is added in front of the numbers to indicate the body of the Constitution, and the letter "A" is added in front to indicate an Amendment. So for example, **C:1.8.7** indicates the Constitution: Article 1, Section 8, Clause 7; while Amendment 20, Section 3, Clause 2 would be written **A:20.3.2**. These are usually in **bold type** (as shown), for ease of reference.

As a final thought, the *Constitution Made Easy* is much easier to understand than the original, but is not intended to replace it for serious study. Almost anyone can read this modern version (the odd-numbered pages) in under 30 minutes, and should be able to grasp the essential propositions and themes. It is hoped that this will then inspire the reader to read and study the original, perhaps using the modern version and footnotes as tools.

The Constitution is "the supreme law of the land." Virtually every elected and public official in America takes an oath to uphold it. The President promises to "preserve, protect and defend" it. The organization chart of the United States Government shows Congress, the President and the Supreme Court *underneath* the Constitution.

The Constitution has been called the greatest governing document ever written by man. Understanding it is worth the effort, and now easier than ever before. Enjoy!

The Constitution of the United States

We the People of the United States, in Order to form a more perfect Union, establish Justice, insure domestic Tranquility, provide for the common defence, promote the general Welfare, and secure the Blessings of Liberty to ourselves and our Posterity, do ordain and establish this Constitution for the United States of America.

Article. I.

Section. 1.

All legislative Powers herein granted shall be vested in a Congress of the United States, which shall consist of a Senate and House of Representatives.

Section. 2.

The House of Representatives shall be composed of Members chosen every second Year by the People of the several States, and the Electors in each State shall have the Qualifications requisite for Electors of the most numerous Branch of the State Legislature.

No Person shall be a Representative who shall not have attained to the Age of twenty five Years, and been seven Years a Citizen of the United States, and who shall not, when elected, be an Inhabitant of that State in which he shall be chosen.

Representatives and direct Taxes shall be apportioned among the several States which may be included within this Union, according to their respective Numbers, which shall be determined by adding to the whole Number of free Persons, including those bound to Service for a Term of Years, and excluding Indians not taxed, three fifths of all other Persons. [Changed by Section 2 of the 14th Amendment, and the 16th Amendment]

The Constitution Made Easy

The Constitution of the United States

We the people of the United States have created and agreed to this Constitution for the United States of America. We have done this in order to make our Union stronger, set standards for justice, keep the peace at home, provide for our common defense, promote our general well-being, and make sure that the blessings of liberty continue for ourselves and our descendents.

Article 1

Section 1

All of the law-making Powers granted by this agreement will be entrusted to a Congress of the United States. Congress will consist of a Senate and a House of Representatives.

Section 2

1.2.1 The members of the House of Representatives will be elected every two years by the people in each of the States. Each State has a standard it uses to decide who is allowed to vote[1] for its own State legislature.[2] This same standard must be used to determine who is allowed to vote for members of the House of Representatives.

1.2.2 A Representative must be at least 25 years old, and a citizen of the United States for seven years. At the time he or she[3] is elected, the Representative must be a resident of the State that elected him or her.

1.2.3[4] The number of Representatives that each State has will be based upon the population of each State. So will direct taxes (except for income tax[5]). For these purposes the population will count everybody except Indians who are not taxpayers. The right to vote may not be denied to any citizen in any State who is at least 18 years old.[6] This includes the right to vote for President and Vice President[7] of the United States, Representatives in Congress, as well as the Governor, judges and legislators of that State. If any State prevents or hinders any eligible person from voting, unless they participated in rebellion or other crime, the number of Representatives that State is entitled to will be reduced in proportion.

The actual Enumeration shall be made within three Years after the first Meeting of the Congress of the United States, and within every subsequent Term of ten Years, in such Manner as they shall by Law direct. The Number of Representatives shall not exceed one for every thirty Thousand, but each State shall have at Least one Representative; and until such enumeration shall be made, the State of New Hampshire shall be entitled to chuse three, Massachusetts eight, Rhode-Island and Providence Plantations one, Connecticut five, New-York six, New Jersey four, Pennsylvania eight, Delaware one, Maryland six, Virginia ten, North Carolina five, South Carolina five, and Georgia three.

When vacancies happen in the Representation from any State, the Executive Authority thereof shall issue Writs of Election to fill such Vacancies.

The House of Representatives shall chuse their Speaker and other Officers; and shall have the sole Power of Impeachment.

Section. 3.
The Senate of the United States shall be composed of two Senators from each State, chosen by the Legislature thereof for six Years; and each Senator shall have one Vote. [Changed by the 17th Amendment]

Immediately after they shall be assembled in Consequence of the first Election, they shall be divided as equally as may be into three Classes. The Seats of the Senators of the first Class shall be vacated at the Expiration of the second Year, of the second Class at the Expiration of the fourth Year, and of the third Class at the Expiration of the sixth Year, so that one third may be chosen every second Year;

and if Vacancies happen by Resignation, or otherwise, during the Recess of the Legislature of any State, the Executive thereof may make temporary Appointments until the next Meeting of the Legislature, which shall then fill such Vacancies. [Changed by the 17th Amendment]

The Constitution Made Easy

1.2.4   The actual census must be taken within three years after the first meeting of the Congress of the United States, and every ten years after that. Congress will determine by Law how the census will be taken. Each State will have at least one Representative, but otherwise not more than one for each 30,000 people.[8] Until the first census is taken the number of Representatives from each State will be New Hampshire three, Massachusetts eight, Rhode Island one, Connecticut five, New York six, New Jersey four, Pennsylvania eight, Delaware one, Maryland six, Virginia ten, North Carolina five, South Carolina five, and Georgia three.

1.2.5   When any Representative does not finish his or her term, the Governor from his or her State must appoint someone for the remainder of that term.

1.2.6   The House of Representatives will choose their Speaker and other officers, and will have the exclusive Power to bring a charge of Impeachment.[9]

Section 3
1.3.1[10] The Senate of the United States will consist of two Senators from each State, elected by the people of that State for six years; and each Senator will have one vote. Each State has a standard it uses to decide who is allowed to vote[11] for its own State legislature. This same standard must be used to determine who is allowed to vote for members of the Senate. [From A;17.1]

1.3.2   After the first election of Senators, and as soon they meet for the first time, they will be divided into three groups. The first term of the first group will end in two years; the first term of the second group will end in four years; and the first term of the third group will end in six years. In this way, one third of the Senate will be elected every two years.

1.3.3[12] When any Senator does not finish his or her term, the Governor from his or her State must set a Special Election to fill the remainder of that term. However, the legislature of that State may give the Governor power to make a temporary appointment that will only last until the position is filled by the Special Election. [From A;17.2]

No Person shall be a Senator who shall not have attained to the Age of thirty Years, and been nine Years a Citizen of the United States, and who shall not, when elected, be an Inhabitant of that State for which he shall be chosen.

The Vice President of the United States shall be President of the Senate, but shall have no Vote, unless they be equally divided.

The Senate shall chuse their other Officers, and also a President pro tempore, in the Absence of the Vice President, or when he shall exercise the Office of President of the United States.

The Senate shall have the sole Power to try all Impeachments. When sitting for that Purpose, they shall be on Oath or Affirmation. When the President of the United States is tried, the Chief Justice shall preside: And no Person shall be convicted without the Concurrence of two thirds of the Members present.

Judgment in Cases of Impeachment shall not extend further than to removal from Office, and disqualification to hold and enjoy any Office of honor, Trust or Profit under the United States: but the Party convicted shall nevertheless be liable and subject to Indictment, Trial, Judgment and Punishment, according to Law.

Section. 4.

The Times, Places and Manner of holding Elections for Senators and Representatives, shall be prescribed in each State by the Legislature thereof; but the Congress may at any time by Law make or alter such Regulations, except as to the Places of chusing Senators.

The Congress shall assemble at least once in every Year, and such Meeting shall be on the first Monday in December, unless they shall by Law appoint a different Day. [Changed by the 20th Amendment]

Section. 5.

Each House shall be the Judge of the Elections, Returns and Qualifications of its own Members, and a Majority of each shall constitute a Quorum to do Business; but a smaller Number may adjourn from day to day, and may be authorized to compel the Attendance of absent Members, in such Manner, and under such Penalties as each House may provide.

The Constitution Made Easy

1.3.4   A Senator must be at least 30 years old, and a citizen of the United States for nine years. At the time he or she is elected, the Senator must be a resident of the State that elected him or her.

1.3.5   The Vice President of the United States will be President[13] of the Senate, but may not vote except to break a tie.

1.3.6   The Senate will choose their other officers, and also a temporary[14] President. He or she will preside[15] only if the Vice President is absent, or when the Vice President is the Acting President of the United States.

1.3.7   The Senate will have the exclusive Power to try all Impeachments.[16] When they are conducting an Impeachment trial they must first swear that they will act impartially.[17] When the President of the United States is tried, the Chief Justice will preside. There will be no conviction unless two-thirds of the members present vote for it.

1.3.8   The most serious consequences of Impeachment will be to remove the person from office, and disqualify him or her from holding any official position under the United States. However, a convicted person may still have other liability, and could be charged, tried, judged and punished according to Law.[18]

Section 4
1.4.1   The times, places and methods of holding elections for Senators and Representatives, will be decided by each State legislature. Congress may override these regulations at any time by Law.[19]

1.4.2   The terms of Congress will end at Noon on January 3rd, and the terms of their successors will then begin. Congress must meet at least once in every year, and that meeting will also begin at Noon on January 3rd, unless that date is changed by Law.[20]

Section 5
1.5.1   Each House will decide its own elections, returns, and qualifications of its own members. Each House must have a majority present for there to be a quorum[21] that can do business. But a smaller number may meet and then adjourn[22] each day, and may be authorized to make the absent members attend. Each House may decide how members can be made to attend, or penalized for not attending.

Each House may determine the Rules of its Proceedings, punish its Members for disorderly Behaviour, and, with the Concurrence of two thirds, expel a Member.

Each House shall keep a Journal of its Proceedings, and from time to time publish the same, excepting such Parts as may in their Judgment require Secrecy; and the Yeas and Nays of the Members of either House on any question shall, at the Desire of one fifth of those Present, be entered on the Journal.

Neither House, during the Session of Congress, shall, without the Consent of the other, adjourn for more than three days, nor to any other Place than that in which the two Houses shall be sitting.

Section. 6.

The Senators and Representatives shall receive a Compensation for their Services, to be ascertained by Law, and paid out of the Treasury of the United States.

They shall in all Cases, except Treason, Felony and Breach of the Peace, be privileged from Arrest during their Attendance at the Session of their respective Houses, and in going to and returning from the same; and for any Speech or Debate in either House, they shall not be questioned in any other Place.

No Senator or Representative shall, during the Time for which he was elected, be appointed to any civil Office under the Authority of the United States, which shall have been created, or the Emoluments whereof shall have been encreased during such time; and no Person holding any Office under the United States, shall be a Member of either House during his Continuance in Office.

Section. 7.

All Bills for raising Revenue shall originate in the House of Representatives; but the Senate may propose or concur with Amendments as on other Bills.

Every Bill which shall have passed the House of Representatives and the Senate, shall, before it become a Law, be presented to the President of the United States: If he approve he shall sign it, but if not he shall return it, with his Objections to that House in which it shall have

1.5.2   Each House may decide the rules of its proceedings, punish its members for disorderly conduct, and expel a member by a two-thirds vote.

1.5.3   Each House must keep a journal of its proceedings, and periodically publish it. They may omit certain parts that they believe require secrecy. One-fifth of those present in either House may require that the "Yes" and "No" votes of the members on any question be recorded in the journal.

1.5.4   When Congress is in session, neither House may adjourn for more than three days without the consent of the other House. The same consent will be required for either House to adjourn to any other location.

Section 6
1.6.1   Senators and Representatives must be paid for their services in an amount set by Law, and paid out of the Treasury of the United States. Any change in their pay will not take effect until after the next election of Representatives.[23]

1.6.2   They may not be arrested while they are attending a session of their respective Houses, or while they are going to or returning from a session, except for treason, felony or disturbing the peace.[24] They may not be arrested because of any speech or debate in either House, and they may not be questioned in any other place.

1.6.3   No Senator or Representative may be appointed to any official position under the authority of the United States during their term in office, if that position was created during their term, or if the pay plan was increased during their term. No person holding any official position under the United States may be a member of either House at the same time that he or she holds this other office.

Section 7
1.7.1   All bills for raising money must originate in the House of Representatives. But the Senate may propose or agree with amendments to these bills, just as it can with other bills.

1.7.2   Every bill which passes the House and Senate must be presented to the President of the United States before it becomes a Law. If the President approves of it, he or she must sign it. If not, the President must return it, along with his or her objections, to the House

originated, who shall enter the Objections at large on their Journal, and proceed to reconsider it.

If after such Reconsideration two thirds of that House shall agree to pass the Bill, it shall be sent, together with the Objections, to the other House, by which it shall likewise be reconsidered, and if approved by two thirds of that House, it shall become a Law.

But in all such Cases the Votes of both Houses shall be determined by yeas and Nays, and the Names of the Persons voting for and against the Bill shall be entered on the Journal of each House respectively. If any Bill shall not be returned by the President within ten Days (Sundays excepted) after it shall have been presented to him, the Same shall be a Law, in like Manner as if he had signed it, unless the Congress by their Adjournment prevent its Return, in which Case it shall not be a Law.

Every Order, Resolution, or Vote to which the Concurrence of the Senate and House of Representatives may be necessary (except on a question of Adjournment) shall be presented to the President of the United States; and before the Same shall take Effect, shall be approved by him, or being disapproved by him, shall be repassed by two thirds of the Senate and House of Representatives, according to the Rules and Limitations prescribed in the Case of a Bill.

Section. 8.
The Congress shall have Power

To lay and collect Taxes, Duties, Imposts and Excises, to pay the Debts and provide for the common Defence and general Welfare of the United States; but all Duties, Imposts and Excises shall be uniform throughout the United States;

To borrow Money on the credit of the United States;

To regulate Commerce with foreign Nations, and among the several States, and with the Indian Tribes;

To establish an uniform Rule of Naturalization, and uniform Laws on the subject of Bankruptcies throughout the United States;

in which it originated. That House must enter the President's objections on their journal, and proceed to reconsider it.

1.7.3 After they reconsider, if two-thirds of that House agrees to pass the bill, it must be sent, together with the objections, to the other House. That House must also reconsider it, and if they approve it by a two-thirds vote, it will become a Law.

1.7.4 In all such cases the votes of both Houses must be determined by saying "Yes" or "No," and the names of the people voting for and against the bill must be entered on the journal of each House respectively. If any bill is not returned by the President within ten days after it has been presented to him or her (not counting Sundays), it will become a Law, just as if he or she had signed it. There is an exception if Congress adjourns in less than ten days, which prevents its return, in which case it will not become Law.

1.7.5 Every other kind of order, resolution, or vote which the Senate and House of Representatives have to both agree on, must be presented to the President of the United States. Before it can take effect, it must be approved by him or her. If the President does not approve it, it must be re-passed by two-thirds of the Senate and House of Representatives in order for it to go into effect. The same rules and limitations apply as in the case of a bill (above). This paragraph does not apply to a vote to adjourn.

Section 8
Congress will have Power:

1.8.1 To assess and collect taxes on imports, exports, and purchases to pay the debts and provide for the common defense and general well-being[25] of the United States. All such taxes must be uniform[26] throughout the United States;

1.8.2 To borrow money on the credit of the United States;

1.8.3 To regulate trade with foreign nations, and among the separate States, and with the Indian tribes;

1.8.4 To establish standard rules for becoming a naturalized citizen,[27] and establish standard Laws about bankruptcy throughout the United States;

To coin Money, regulate the Value thereof, and of foreign Coin, and fix the Standard of Weights and Measures;

To provide for the Punishment of counterfeiting the Securities and current Coin of the United States;

To establish Post Offices and post Roads;

To promote the Progress of Science and useful Arts, by securing for limited Times to Authors and Inventors the exclusive Right to their respective Writings and Discoveries;

To constitute Tribunals inferior to the supreme Court;

To define and punish Piracies and Felonies committed on the high Seas, and Offences against the Law of Nations;

To declare War, grant Letters of Marque and Reprisal, and make Rules concerning Captures on Land and Water;

To raise and support Armies, but no Appropriation of Money to that Use shall be for a longer Term than two Years;

To provide and maintain a Navy;

To make Rules for the Government and Regulation of the land and naval Forces;

To provide for calling forth the Militia to execute the Laws of the Union, suppress Insurrections and repel Invasions;

To provide for organizing, arming, and disciplining, the Militia, and for governing such Part of them as may be employed in the Service of the United States, reserving to the States respectively, the Appointment of the Officers, and the Authority of training the Militia according to the discipline prescribed by Congress;

To exercise exclusive Legislation in all Cases whatsoever, over such District (not exceeding ten Miles square) as may, by Cession of particular States, and the Acceptance of Congress, become the Seat of the Government of the United States, and to exercise like Authority over all Places purchased by the Consent of the Legislature of the State in

The Constitution Made Easy

1.8.5 To coin money, decide the value of it, decide the value of foreign money, and set the standard of weights and measures;

1.8.6 To decide the punishment for counterfeiting the money and other valuables of the United States;

1.8.7 To establish post offices and post roads;

1.8.8 To promote the progress of science and useful arts, by making sure that authors and inventors have ownership of their writings and discoveries for a certain period of time;

1.8.9 To create courts underneath the Supreme Court;

1.8.10 To define and punish piracy, felonies committed on the high seas, and international crimes;

1.8.11 To declare war, grant letters of retaliation,[28] and make rules concerning captures[29] on land and water;

1.8.12 To raise and support Armies. But Congress may not allocate money for this purpose for more than two years at a time;

1.8.13 To provide and maintain a Navy;

1.8.14 To make rules that govern and regulate the land and naval forces;

1.8.15 To provide for calling upon the Militia[30] to enforce the Laws of the Union, put down rebellions and repel invasions;

1.8.16 To provide for organizing, arming, and disciplining the Militia, and for governing any part of them that are serving the United States at the time. The States will still appoint the officers, and have the authority to train the Militia according to the standards prescribed by Congress;

1.8.17 To make all Laws whatsoever for the District that will be the headquarters of the Government of the United States (Washington, D.C.).[31] This District will not be more than ten miles square, and will consist of land granted by one or more States and accepted by Congress. Congress will have the same authority over forts, storage places for weapons and ammunition, dock-yards[32] and other

which the Same shall be, for the Erection of Forts, Magazines, Arsenals, dock-Yards, and other needful Buildings;--And

To make all Laws which shall be necessary and proper for carrying into Execution the foregoing Powers, and all other Powers vested by this Constitution in the Government of the United States, or in any Department or Officer thereof.

Section. 9.
The Migration or Importation of such Persons as any of the States now existing shall think proper to admit, shall not be prohibited by the Congress prior to the Year one thousand eight hundred and eight, but a Tax or duty may be imposed on such Importation, not exceeding ten dollars for each Person.

The Privilege of the Writ of Habeas Corpus shall not be suspended, unless when in Cases of Rebellion or Invasion the public Safety may require it.

No Bill of Attainder or ex post facto Law shall be passed.

No Capitation, or other direct, Tax shall be laid, unless in Proportion to the Census or enumeration herein before directed to be taken. [Changed by the 16th Amendment]
No Tax or Duty shall be laid on Articles exported from any State.

No Preference shall be given by any Regulation of Commerce or Revenue to the Ports of one State over those of another; nor shall Vessels bound to, or from, one State, be obliged to enter, clear, or pay Duties in another.

No Money shall be drawn from the Treasury, but in Consequence of Appropriations made by Law; and a regular Statement and Account of the Receipts and Expenditures of all public Money shall be published from time to time.
No Title of Nobility shall be granted by the United States: And no Person holding any Office of Profit or Trust under them, shall, without the Consent of the Congress, accept of any present, Emolument, Office, or Title, of any kind whatever, from any King, Prince, or foreign State.

necessary buildings. These places must first be purchased with the consent of the legislature of the State where they are located; and

1.8.18 To make all Laws which are necessary and proper for executing the Powers listed above, and all other Powers granted by this Constitution to the Government of the United States, or to any department or officer of it.

Section 9[33]

1.9.1 The existing States may allow any people they wish to be admitted or imported. Congress may not prohibit this before the year 1808, but may impose a tax of up to ten dollars per person. [This clause was changed by Law on January 1, 1808.[34]]

1.9.2 The right of any arrested person to be seen by an impartial judge[35] may not be suspended. There may be exceptions only during a rebellion or invasion if the public safety requires it.

1.9.3 No Law may be passed which pronounces a person guilty of a crime,[36] or which is retroactive.[37]

1.9.4 No direct taxes may be assessed unless they are in proportion to the census. There is an exception for income tax.[38]

1.9.5 No tax may be assessed on goods exported from any State.

1.9.6 No preference may be given to the ports of one State over those of another by regulating the trade or taxes. Ships bound to or from one State, may not be required to enter, stop at, or pay taxes in another.

1.9.7 No money may be taken out of the Treasury, except the amounts that have been allocated by Law. A financial statement showing where this money came from, and how it was spent, must be made available to the public on a regular basis.

1.9.8 No title of nobility may be granted by the United States.[39] No person who holds any official position under them may accept any gift, money, office, or title of any kind whatever; from any king, prince or foreign State, without the consent of Congress.

Section. 10.

No State shall enter into any Treaty, Alliance, or Confederation; grant Letters of Marque and Reprisal;

coin Money; emit Bills of Credit; make any Thing but gold and silver Coin a Tender in Payment of Debts;

pass any Bill of Attainder, ex post facto Law,

or Law impairing the Obligation of Contracts, or grant any Title of Nobility.

No State shall, without the Consent of the Congress, lay any Imposts or Duties on Imports or Exports, except what may be absolutely necessary for executing it's inspection Laws: and the net Produce of all Duties and Imposts, laid by any State on Imports or Exports, shall be for the Use of the Treasury of the United States; and all such Laws shall be subject to the Revision and Controul of the Congress.

No State shall, without the Consent of Congress, lay any Duty of Tonnage, keep Troops, or Ships of War in time of Peace, enter into any Agreement or Compact with another State, or with a foreign Power, or engage in War, unless actually invaded, or in such imminent Danger as will not admit of delay.

Article. II.

Section. 1.

The executive Power shall be vested in a President of the United States of America. He shall hold his Office during the Term of four Years, and, together with the Vice President, chosen for the same Term, be elected, as follows:

Each State shall appoint, in such Manner as the Legislature thereof may direct, a Number of Electors, equal to the whole Number of Senators and Representatives to which the State may be entitled in the Congress: but no Senator or Representative, or Person holding an Office of Trust or Profit under the United States, shall be appointed an Elector.

The Constitution Made Easy

Section 10[40]

1.10.1 No State may enter into any treaty, alliance, or confederation; or grant letters of retaliation.[41]

1.10.2 (No State may) coin money, print paper money, or make anything except gold and silver coin a method of paying debts.

1.10.3 (No State may) pass any Law which pronounces a person guilty of a crime,[42] or which is retroactive.[43]

1.10.4 (No State may) pass any Law that interferes with private contracts, or grant any title of nobility.

1.10.5 The consent of Congress is required before any State may assess any tax on imports or exports, except what is absolutely necessary for executing it's inspection Laws. The net proceeds of all these taxes will be for the use of the Treasury of the United States, and all such Laws will be subject to the revision and control of Congress.

1.10.6 The consent of Congress is required before any State may assess any tax based on the weight of shipments, or keep troops or warships in time of peace, or enter into any agreement or compact with another State or foreign Power, or engage in war. There is an exception for engaging in war if a State is actually invaded, or is in such immediate danger that it does not dare to wait.

Article 2

Section 1

2.1.1 The executive Power will be entrusted to a President of the United States of America. He or she will hold his or her office for a term of four years, not to exceed two terms.[44] Each term will begin and end at Noon on January 20th.[45] The President and Vice President will be elected to the same term as follows:

2.1.2 Each State, (and Washington, D.C.[46]), must appoint a number of electors equal to the total number of Senators and Representatives which that State (or District) is entitled to in Congress. The legislature of each State may determine the manner in which the electors are chosen. No Senator or Representative, or person holding an official position under the United States, may be appointed as an elector.

The Electors shall meet in their respective States, and vote by Ballot for two Persons, of whom one at least shall not be an Inhabitant of the same State with themselves. [Changed by the 12th Amendment]

And they shall make a List of all the Persons voted for, and of the Number of Votes for each; which List they shall sign and certify, and transmit sealed to the Seat of the Government of the United States, directed to the President of the Senate. [Changed by the 12th Amendment]

The President of the Senate shall, in the Presence of the Senate and House of Representatives, open all the Certificates, and the Votes shall then be counted. The Person having the greatest Number of Votes shall be the President, if such Number be a Majority of the whole Number of Electors appointed; [Changed by the 12th Amendment]

and if there be more than one who have such Majority, and have an equal Number of Votes, then the House of Representatives shall immediately chuse by Ballot one of them for President; and if no Person have a Majority, then from the five highest on the List the said House shall in like Manner chuse the President. But in chusing the President, the Votes shall be taken by States, the Representation from each State having one Vote; A quorum for this purpose shall consist of a Member or Members from two thirds of the States, and a Majority of all the States shall be necessary to a Choice. [Changed by the 12th Amendment]

[See Section 3 of Amendment 20]

[See Section 3 of Amendment 20]

The Constitution Made Easy

2.1.3[47] The electors must meet in their respective States, and vote by ballot for President and Vice President. They may not vote for a President and a Vice President who are both from the same State as the electors. [From A:12.1]

2.1.4 They must name in one set of ballots the person they voted for as President, and in a different set of ballots the person they voted for as Vice President. They must make separate lists of all the persons they voted for as President, and of all persons they voted for as Vice President, and the number of votes for each. They must sign these lists, and certify that they are correct, and send them sealed to the President of the Senate. [From A:12.2]

2.1.5 The President of the Senate must open all the certificates in the presence of the Senate and House of Representatives, and the votes must then be counted. The person receiving the greatest number of votes for President will become the President, as long as he or she receives a majority of the total number of electors. [From A:12.3]

2.1.6 If no person receives a majority, then the House of Representatives must immediately elect the President by ballot. They must choose him or her from the three persons with the highest numbers of votes. In choosing the President, the votes must be taken by States, and each State will have one vote. A quorum for this purpose will consist of at least one member from two-thirds of the States, and a majority of all the States will be necessary for the election to be final. [From A:12.4]

2.1.7 If the President elect dies before the beginning of his or her term (Noon, January 20th), then the Vice President elect will become President. If a President has not been chosen before the beginning of his or her term, or if the President elect does not qualify, then the Vice President elect will act as President until a qualified President is chosen. [From A:12.5 and A:20.3.1]

2.1.8 In case neither a President elect, nor a Vice President elect qualifies, Congress may provide for this by law. Then this law will determine who will act as President, or the way in which the Acting President will be selected. This person will act as President until a qualified President or Vice President is chosen. [From A:12.6 and A:20.3.2]

In every Case, after the Choice of the President, the Person having the greatest Number of Votes of the Electors shall be the Vice President. But if there should remain two or more who have equal Votes, the Senate shall chuse from them by Ballot the Vice President. [Changed by the 12th Amendment]

The Congress may determine the Time of chusing the Electors, and the Day on which they shall give their Votes; which Day shall be the same throughout the United States.

No Person except a natural born Citizen, or a Citizen of the United States, at the time of the Adoption of this Constitution, shall be eligible to the Office of President; neither shall any Person be eligible to that Office who shall not have attained to the Age of thirty five Years, and been fourteen Years a Resident within the United States.

In Case of the Removal of the President from Office, or of his Death, Resignation, or Inability to discharge the Powers and Duties of the said Office, the Same shall devolve on the Vice President, [Changed by the 25th Amendment]

[See Amendment 25]

and the Congress may by Law provide for the Case of Removal, Death, Resignation or Inability, both of the President and Vice President, declaring what Officer shall then act as President, and such Officer shall act accordingly, until the Disability be removed, or a President shall be elected. [*The whole paragraph (above) was underlined in the original; but a portion has been retained in this version as there is no replacement language in the 25th Amendment, or any other Amendment. See 2.1.14 and footnote.]

[See Amendment 25]

The Constitution Made Easy

2.1.9   The person receiving the greatest number of votes for Vice President will become the Vice President, as long as he or she receives a majority of the total number of electors. If no person receives a majority, then the Senate must choose the Vice President from the two persons with the highest numbers of votes. A quorum for this purpose will consist of two-thirds of the total number of Senators, and a majority of the total number will be necessary for the election to be final. If a person is not eligible, under the Constitution, to be President of the United States, that person will not be eligible to be Vice President either. [From A:12.7]

2.1.10   Congress may determine the time of choosing the electors, and the day on which they must cast their votes. This day must be the same throughout the United States.

2.1.11   To be eligible for the office of President, a person must be a natural-born citizen (or else a citizen at the time this Constitution was adopted). He or she must also be at least 35 years old and a resident within the United States for fourteen years.

2.1.12[48]   In case of the removal of the President from office, or of his or her death or resignation, the Vice President will become President. [From A:25.1]

2.1.13   Whenever there is a vacancy in the office of the Vice President, the President must nominate a new Vice President. He will take office upon confirmation by a majority vote of both Houses of Congress. [From A:25.2]

2.1.14   In case the President and Vice President are both removed from office, or have died, or have resigned, or have become unable to discharge the powers and duties of office, Congress may provide for this by law. Then this law will determine who will act as President until one of them is able to resume their office, or until a new President is elected.[49]

2.1.15   Whenever the President believes that he or she is unable to discharge the powers and duties of office, he or she may send written declaration to the temporary President of the Senate and to the Speaker of the House of Representatives. Until the President sends them a written declaration that he or she has become able again, these powers and duties must be discharged by the Vice President as Acting President. [From A:25.3]

[See Amendment 25]

[See Amendment 25]

[See Amendment 25]

The President shall, at stated Times, receive for his Services, a Compensation, which shall neither be increased nor diminished during the Period for which he shall have been elected, and he shall not receive within that Period any other Emolument from the United States, or any of them.

Before he enter on the Execution of his Office, he shall take the following Oath or Affirmation:--"I do solemnly swear (or affirm) that I will faithfully execute the Office of President of the United States, and will to the best of my Ability, preserve, protect and defend the Constitution of the United States."

The Constitution Made Easy

2.1.16 Whenever the Vice President and a majority of the Cabinet officers[50] agree that the President is unable to discharge the powers and duties of office, they may send their written declaration to the temporary President of the Senate and the Speaker of the House of Representatives. Then the Vice President must immediately assume the powers and duties as Acting President. (Congress may change this in the future from "the Cabinet" to some other group they designate by law.) [From A:25.4]

2.1.17 After this, if the President believes that no inability exists, he or she must send written declaration to the temporary President of the Senate and to the Speaker of the House of Representatives. The President will resume the powers and duties of office unless the Vice President and a majority of the Cabinet officers oppose him or her. If they do, they must send their written declaration within four days to the temporary President of the Senate and to the Speaker of the House of Representatives reasserting that the President is unable to discharge the powers and duties of office. [From A:25.5]

2.1.18 At this point Congress must decide the issue. They must meet within 48 hours for this purpose if they are not already in session. Congress must make a determination within 21 days of receiving the most recent declaration (or 23 days if they were not in session). If Congress determines that the President is unable to discharge the powers and duties of office, then the Vice President will continue as Acting President. They must do this by two-thirds vote of both Houses. Otherwise, the President will resume the powers and duties of his or her office. [From A:25.6]

2.1.19 The President must be paid on a regular basis. This pay may not be increased nor decreased during his or her term in office. During this term, the President may not receive any other payment from the United States, or any of them.

2.1.20 Before the President actually exercises any of the powers or duties of office, he or she must take the following Oath or Affirmation: "I do solemnly swear (or affirm) that I will faithfully execute the office of President of the United States, and will to the best of my ability, preserve, protect and defend the Constitution of the United States."

Section. 2.

    The President shall be Commander in Chief of the Army and Navy of the United States, and of the Militia of the several States, when called into the actual Service of the United States; he may require the Opinion, in writing, of the principal Officer in each of the executive Departments, upon any Subject relating to the Duties of their respective Offices, and he shall have Power to grant Reprieves and Pardons for Offences against the United States, except in Cases of Impeachment.

    He shall have Power, by and with the Advice and Consent of the Senate, to make Treaties, provided two thirds of the Senators present concur; and he shall nominate, and by and with the Advice and Consent of the Senate, shall appoint Ambassadors, other public Ministers and Consuls, Judges of the supreme Court, and all other Officers of the United States, whose Appointments are not herein otherwise provided for, and which shall be established by Law:

but the Congress may by Law vest the Appointment of such inferior Officers, as they think proper, in the President alone, in the Courts of Law, or in the Heads of Departments.

    The President shall have Power to fill up all Vacancies that may happen during the Recess of the Senate, by granting Commissions which shall expire at the End of their next Session.

Section. 3.

    He shall from time to time give to the Congress Information of the State of the Union, and recommend to their Consideration such Measures as he shall judge necessary and expedient;

he may, on extraordinary Occasions, convene both Houses, or either of them, and in Case of Disagreement between them, with Respect to the Time of Adjournment, he may adjourn them to such Time as he shall think proper;

he shall receive Ambassadors and other public Ministers; he shall take Care that the Laws be faithfully executed, and shall Commission all the Officers of the United States.

The Constitution Made Easy

Section 2

2.2.1   The President will be Commander in Chief of the Army and Navy of the United States, and of the Militia of the separate States, when they are called into the actual service of the United States. The President may require the written opinion of the Cabinet officers upon any subject relating to the duties of their respective offices. He or she will have Power to grant reprieves and pardons for offenses against the United States, except in cases of Impeachment.

2.2.2   The President will have Power to make treaties with the advice and consent of the Senate. Two-thirds of the Senators present must agree. He or she must nominate and then appoint ambassadors, public officials, diplomats, Judges of the Supreme Court, and all other officers of the United States. This includes any appointments that are not provided for elsewhere in the Constitution, but are later established by Law. These appointments also require the advice and consent of the Senate.

2.2.3   But Congress may give the President the Power to appoint some lower-ranking officers by himself or herself. Congress may give the same power to the courts of Law, or the heads of departments. They would do this by Law, as they think it is proper.

2.2.4   The President will have Power to fill up all vacancies that may happen during the recess of the Senate, by granting commissions which will expire at the end of their next session.

Section 3

2.3.1   The President must regularly give information to Congress concerning the State of the Union, and recommend for their consideration whatever measures he or she thinks are necessary and expedient.

2.3.2   On extraordinary occasions, the President may convene one or both Houses of Congress. In cases when the two Houses disagree about when to adjourn, the President may adjourn them to the time he or she thinks is proper.

2.3.3   The President must receive ambassadors and other public officials. He or she must make sure that the Laws are faithfully carried out, and must commission all the officers of the United States.

Section. 4.

The President, Vice President and all civil Officers of the United States, shall be removed from Office on Impeachment for, and Conviction of, Treason, Bribery, or other high Crimes and Misdemeanors.

Article III.

Section. 1.

The judicial Power of the United States shall be vested in one supreme Court, and in such inferior Courts as the Congress may from time to time ordain and establish. The Judges, both of the supreme and inferior Courts, shall hold their Offices during good Behaviour, and shall, at stated Times, receive for their Services a Compensation, which shall not be diminished during their Continuance in Office.

Section. 2.

The judicial Power shall extend to all Cases, in Law and Equity, arising under this Constitution, the Laws of the United States, and Treaties made, or which shall be made, under their Authority;--to all Cases affecting Ambassadors, other public Ministers and Consuls;--to all Cases of admiralty and maritime Jurisdiction;--to Controversies to which the United States shall be a Party;--to Controversies between two or more States;-- between a State and Citizens of another State;--between Citizens of different States;--between Citizens of the same State claiming Lands under Grants of different States, and between a State, or the Citizens thereof, and foreign States, Citizens or Subjects. [Changed by the 11th Amendment.]

In all Cases affecting Ambassadors, other public Ministers and Consuls, and those in which a State shall be Party, the supreme Court shall have original Jurisdiction. In all the other Cases before mentioned, the supreme Court shall have appellate Jurisdiction, both as to Law and Fact, with such Exceptions, and under such Regulations as the Congress shall make.

The Trial of all Crimes, except in Cases of Impeachment, shall be by Jury; and such Trial shall be held in the State where the said Crimes shall have been committed; but when not committed within any State, the Trial shall be at such Place or Places as the Congress may by Law have directed.

The Constitution Made Easy

Section 4

The President, Vice President and all government officials of the United States, must be removed from office if they are Impeached for, and then convicted of, treason, bribery, or other felonies or misdemeanors.

Article 3

Section 1

The judicial Power of the United States, will be entrusted to one Supreme Court, and in whatever lower courts Congress decides to create in the future. The Judges of all these courts may stay in office for as long as they demonstrate good behavior. They must be paid for their services on a regular basis, and their pay may not be decreased during their time in office.

Section 2

3.2.1 The judicial Power will include all civil and criminal cases that concern this Constitution, the Laws of the United States, and treaties made under their authority. The judicial Power will also include all cases affecting ambassadors, other public officers and diplomats, and all cases where the Laws of the oceans and seas apply. The judicial Power will also include all controversies in which the United States is one of the parties, all controversies between two or more States, between citizens of different States, and between citizens of the same State who are claiming lands under grants of different States.[51]

3.2.2 The Supreme Court will have primary authority over all cases that affect ambassadors, other public officials and diplomats, and those cases in which a State is involved. The Supreme Court will have authority in all of the other cases previously mentioned if the cases are appealed to them. This authority will include both matters of Law and fact. There may be exceptions under regulations that Congress makes.

3.2.3 Trials for all crimes, except cases of Impeachment, must be by jury; and these trials must be held in the State where the crimes were committed. If the crimes were not committed inside of any State, the trial will be held wherever Congress has decided by Law.

Section. 3.

Treason against the United States, shall consist only in levying War against them, or in adhering to their Enemies, giving them Aid and Comfort. No Person shall be convicted of Treason unless on the Testimony of two Witnesses to the same overt Act, or on Confession in open Court.

The Congress shall have Power to declare the Punishment of Treason, but no Attainder of Treason shall work Corruption of Blood, or Forfeiture except during the Life of the Person attainted.

Article. IV.

Section. 1.

Full Faith and Credit shall be given in each State to the public Acts, Records, and judicial Proceedings of every other State. And the Congress may by general Laws prescribe the Manner in which such Acts, Records and Proceedings shall be proved, and the Effect thereof.

Section. 2.

The Citizens of each State shall be entitled to all Privileges and Immunities of Citizens in the several States.

A Person charged in any State with Treason, Felony, or other Crime, who shall flee from Justice, and be found in another State, shall on Demand of the executive Authority of the State from which he fled, be delivered up, to be removed to the State having Jurisdiction of the Crime.

No Person held to Service or Labour in one State, under the Laws thereof, escaping into another, shall, in Consequence of any Law or Regulation therein, be discharged from such Service or Labour, but shall be delivered up on Claim of the Party to whom such Service or Labour may be due. [Changed by the 13th Amendment]

Section. 3.

New States may be admitted by the Congress into this Union; but no new State shall be formed or erected within the Jurisdiction of any other State; nor any State be formed by the Junction of two or more States, or Parts of States, without the Consent of the Legislatures of the States concerned as well as of the Congress.

Section 3

3.3.1   Treason against the United States means making war against them, or joining with their enemies, or giving them assistance and support. A person may not be convicted of treason unless there is testimony of at least two witnesses to the same actual act, or unless the person confesses in a public courtroom.

3.3.2   Congress will have Power to declare the punishment for treason, but the penalty may not include confiscating a person's property after that person is executed.[52]

Article 4

Section 1

Each State must fully accept the public acts, records, and court actions of every other State. Congress may write general Laws[53] that describe how these acts, records and court actions can be proven, and what effect they will have.

Section 2

4.2.1   The citizens of each State will be entitled to all the privileges and freedoms of citizens in the other States.

4.2.2   If a person is charged with treason, felony, or other crime in one State, then flees to another State and is found there, then this fugitive must be returned to the State he or she fled from, if the executive authority from that State demands it.

[Made obsolete by the 13th Amendment[54]]

Section 3

4.3.1   New States may be admitted into this Union by Congress. But no new State may be formed or created within the boundaries of any other State unless it is approved by Congress and the legislature of the State affected. And no new State may be formed by combining two or more States, or parts of those States, unless it is approved by Congress and the legislatures of the States affected.

The Congress shall have Power to dispose of and make all needful Rules and Regulations respecting the Territory or other Property belonging to the United States; and nothing in this Constitution shall be so construed as to Prejudice any Claims of the United States, or of any particular State.

Section. 4.

The United States shall guarantee to every State in this Union a Republican Form of Government, and shall protect each of them against Invasion; and on Application of the Legislature, or of the Executive (when the Legislature cannot be convened), against domestic Violence.

Article. V.

The Congress, whenever two thirds of both Houses shall deem it necessary, shall propose Amendments to this Constitution, or, on the Application of the Legislatures of two thirds of the several States, shall call a Convention for proposing Amendments,

which, in either Case, shall be valid to all Intents and Purposes, as Part of this Constitution, when ratified by the Legislatures of three fourths of the several States, or by Conventions in three fourths thereof, as the one or the other Mode of Ratification may be proposed by the Congress;

Provided that no Amendment which may be made prior to the Year One thousand eight hundred and eight shall in any Manner affect the first and fourth Clauses in the Ninth Section of the first Article; and that no State, without its Consent, shall be deprived of its equal Suffrage in the Senate.

4.3.2   Congress will have Power to sell or transfer the territory or other property belonging to the United States, and to make all necessary rules and regulations for them. But nothing in this Constitution may be interpreted in a way that it gives any State, or the United States, any preference concerning claims they may have.

Section 4

The United States will guarantee a Republican form of Government to every State in this Union, and will protect each of them from invasion. They will also be protected from domestic violence if the legislature of a State requests it. If the legislature cannot be convened, the Governor of that State may request it.

Article 5

Section 1

Amendments to this Constitution may be proposed in two different ways. The first way is for Congress to propose them whenever two-thirds of both Houses decide it is necessary. The second way is for the legislatures of two-thirds of the States to request it, and then Congress must call a convention for proposing Amendments.

Section 2

There are also two different ways for the proposed Amendments to receive final approval[55] and Congress will propose one. The first way is for three-fourths of the State legislatures to approve them. The second way is for conventions in three-fourths of the States to approve them. If they are approved, these Amendments will become an actual part of the Constitution.

Section 3

No Amendment may be made before the year 1808 which affects **C:1.9.1 or 1.9.4** of this Constitution in any way. No State may ever be deprived of equal representation in the Senate without its consent.

Article. VI.

All Debts contracted and Engagements entered into, before the Adoption of this Constitution, shall be as valid against the United States under this Constitution, as under the Confederation.

This Constitution, and the Laws of the United States which shall be made in Pursuance thereof; and all Treaties made, or which shall be made, under the Authority of the United States, shall be the supreme Law of the Land; and the Judges in every State shall be bound thereby, any Thing in the Constitution or Laws of any State to the Contrary notwithstanding.

The Senators and Representatives before mentioned, and the Members of the several State Legislatures, and all executive and judicial Officers, both of the United States and of the several States, shall be bound by Oath or Affirmation, to support this Constitution; but no religious Test shall ever be required as a Qualification to any Office or public Trust under the United States.

Article. VII.

The Ratification of the Conventions of nine States, shall be sufficient for the Establishment of this Constitution between the States so ratifying the Same.

Done in Convention by the Unanimous Consent of the States present the Seventeenth Day of September in the Year of our Lord one thousand seven hundred and Eighty seven and of the Independence of the United States of America the Twelfth In witness whereof We have hereunto subscribed our Names,

G . Washington--President and deputy from Virginia

Attest William Jackson Secretary

Delaware   Geo: Read, Gunning Bedford jun, John Dickinson, Richard Bassett Jaco: Broom

The Constitution Made Easy

Article 6

Section 1
All debts that have been incurred, and all agreements that have been made, before this Constitution becomes effective, will be just as binding upon the United States under this Constitution, as they were under the Confederation.[56]

Section 2
This Constitution will be the supreme Law of the land. So are the Laws of the United States which are made that conform with it. So are all treaties made by the authority of the United States in the past, and in the future. Judges in every State will be bound by them. Nothing in any State Law or State Constitution which is different may stand against them.

Section 3
All Senators and Representatives, and every member of every State legislature, and all executive and judicial officers of the United States, and of every State, will be bound by Oath or Affirmation, to support this Constitution. But no religious test may ever be required as a qualification for any official position under the United States.

Article 7

Approval by the Conventions of nine States will be enough for establishing this Constitution between the States that approve it.

This has been done in convention, by the unanimous consent of the States who are present, on September 17th, in the Year of our Lord 1787, which is also the twelfth year of the Independence of the United States of America. As witnesses of this we have signed our Names as follows:

George Washington--President and deputy from Virginia

Attest William Jackson Secretary

Delaware: George Read, Gunning Bedford, Jr., John Dickinson, Richard Bassett, Jacob Broom

The Constitution of the United States

Maryland James McHenry, Dan of St Thos. Jenifer, Danl Carroll

Virginia John Blair, James Madison Jr.

North Carolina Wm. Blount, Richd. Dobbs Spaight, Hu Williamson

South Carolina J. Rutledge, Charles Cotesworth Pinckney, Charles Pinckney, Pierce Butler

Georgia William Few, Abr Baldwin

New Hampshire John Langdon, Nicholas Gilman

Massachusetts Nathaniel Gorham, Rufus King

Connecticut Wm. Saml. Johnson, Roger Sherman

New York Alexander Hamilton

New Jersey Wil: Livingston, David Brearley, Wm. Paterson, Jona: Dayton

Pennsylvania B Franklin, Thomas Mifflin, Robt Morris, Geo. Clymer, Thos. FitzSimons, Jared Ingersoll, James Wilson, Gouv Morris

Text of Constitution taken from:
http://www.archives.gov/exhibits/charters/constitution_transcript.html
Retrieved August 3, 2011

The Constitution Made Easy

Maryland: James McHenry, Daniel of St. Thomas Jenifer, Daniel Carroll

Virginia: John Blair, James Madison Jr.

North Carolina: William Blount, Richard Dobbs Spaight, Hugh Williamson

South Carolina: John Rutledge, Charles Cotesworth Pinckney, Charles Pinckney, Pierce Butler

Georgia: William Few, Abraham Baldwin

New Hampshire: John Langdon, Nicholas Gilman

Massachusetts: Nathaniel Gorham, Rufus King

Connecticut: William Samuel Johnson, Roger Sherman

New York: Alexander Hamilton

New Jersey: William Livingston, David Brearley, William Paterson, Jonathan Dayton

Pennsylvania: Benjamin Franklin, Thomas Mifflin, Robert Morris, George Clymer, Thomas FitzSimons, Jared Ingersoll, James Wilson, Gouvernor Morris

The Constitution of the United States

The Bill of Rights

Preamble

Congress of the United States
begun and held at the City of New-York, on
Wednesday the fourth of March, one thousand seven hundred and eighty
nine.

THE Conventions of a number of the States, having at the time of their
adopting the Constitution, expressed a desire, in order to prevent
misconstruction or abuse of its powers, that further declaratory and
restrictive clauses should be added: And as extending the ground of
public confidence in the Government, will best ensure the beneficent
ends of its institution.

RESOLVED by the Senate and House of Representatives of the United
States of America, in Congress assembled, two thirds of both Houses
concurring, that the following Articles be proposed to the Legislatures of
the several States, as amendments to the Constitution of the United
States, all, or any of which Articles, when ratified by three fourths of the
said Legislatures, to be valid to all intents and purposes, as part of the
said Constitution; viz.

ARTICLES in addition to, and Amendment of the Constitution of the
United States of America, proposed by Congress, and ratified by the
Legislatures of the several States, pursuant to the fifth Article of the
original Constitution.

*Note: The following text is a transcription of the first ten amendments to
the Constitution in their original form. These amendments were ratified
December 15, 1791, and form what is known as the "Bill of Rights."*

Amendment I

Congress shall make no law respecting an establishment of
religion, or prohibiting the free exercise thereof; or abridging the
freedom of speech, or of the press; or the right of the people peaceably to
assemble, and to petition the Government for a redress of grievances.

The Constitution Made Easy

The Bill of Rights[57]

Preamble

(The following is presented by the) Congress of the United States, which convened in New York City on Wednesday, March 4, 1789.

At the time that they adopted the Constitution, several of the State Conventions expressed a desire that further declarations and restrictions should be added in order to prevent misinterpretation or abuse of the Constitution's powers. Since doing so will increase the basis for public confidence in the Government, and is the best way to make sure that the results of establishing it are beneficial;

It is RESOLVED by the Senate and the House of Representatives of the United States of America, while assembled in Congress, and agreed to by two-thirds of both Houses, that the following Articles are to be proposed to the legislatures of the various States. Any of these Articles that are approved by three-fourths of the State legislatures will become Amendments to the Constitution, and will become valid as an actual part of the Constitution.

The following ARTICLES are in addition to, and Amendments of, the Constitution of the United States of America. They have been proposed by Congress and approved by the legislatures of the various States, as required by Article Five of the original Constitution.

Amendment 1

Congress may not make any law that sets up any religion, or interferes with any religious practice. Congress may not make any law that diminishes the freedom of speech, or the freedom of the press, or the right of the people to assemble peacefully, or the right of the people to petition the Government to make things right if it has caused them harm.

Amendment II

A well regulated Militia, being necessary to the security of a free State, the right of the people to keep and bear Arms, shall not be infringed.

Amendment III

No Soldier shall, in time of peace be quartered in any house, without the consent of the Owner, nor in time of war, but in a manner to be prescribed by law.

Amendment IV

The right of the people to be secure in their persons, houses, papers, and effects, against unreasonable searches and seizures, shall not be violated, and no Warrants shall issue, but upon probable cause, supported by Oath or affirmation, and particularly describing the place to be searched, and the persons or things to be seized.

Amendment V

No person shall be held to answer for a capital, or otherwise infamous crime, unless on a presentment or indictment of a Grand Jury, except in cases arising in the land or naval forces, or in the Militia, when in actual service in time of War or public danger;

nor shall any person be subject for the same offence to be twice put in jeopardy of life or limb; nor shall be compelled in any criminal case to be a witness against himself, nor be deprived of life, liberty, or property, without due process of law; nor shall private property be taken for public use, without just compensation.

The Constitution Made Easy

Amendment 2

The people have the right to own and carry firearms,[58] and it may not be violated because a well-equipped Militia[59] is necessary for a State to remain secure and free.

Amendment 3

Soldiers may not be housed in private homes in peacetime unless the owner gives his consent. Soldiers may only be housed in private homes in wartime in a way that will be described by law.

Amendment 4

The people have the right to be protected from unreasonable searches and seizures, and it may not be violated. This protection includes their persons, houses, papers and belongings. No warrant may be issued unless it is reasonably believed that a crime was most likely committed.[60] This belief must be supported by a sworn statement[61] and the warrant must specifically describe the place to be searched, and the persons or things to be seized.

Amendment 5

Nobody may be tried for a crime that might be punishable by death, or for any other terrible crime, unless they are first indicted by a Grand Jury. The exceptions are cases involving the Army or Navy, and cases involving the Militia when they are actually serving during time of war or public danger.

Nobody may be tried twice for the same crime if the penalty could include loss of life or limb.[62] Nobody may be forced to testify against himself or herself in any criminal case. Nobody may be deprived of life, liberty, or property without proper operation of law. No private property may be taken for public use without fair compensation.

Amendment VI

In all criminal prosecutions, the accused shall enjoy the right to a speedy and public trial, by an impartial jury of the State and district wherein the crime shall have been committed, which district shall have been previously ascertained by law, and to be informed of the nature and cause of the accusation; to be confronted with the witnesses against him; to have compulsory process for obtaining witnesses in his favor, and to have the Assistance of Counsel for his defence.

Amendment VII

In Suits at common law, where the value in controversy shall exceed twenty dollars, the right of trial by jury shall be preserved, and no fact tried by a jury, shall be otherwise re-examined in any Court of the United States, than according to the rules of the common law.

Amendment VIII

Excessive bail shall not be required, nor excessive fines imposed, nor cruel and unusual punishments inflicted.

Amendment IX

The enumeration in the Constitution, of certain rights, shall not be construed to deny or disparage others retained by the people.

Amendment X

The powers not delegated to the United States by the Constitution, nor prohibited by it to the States, are reserved to the States respectively, or to the people.

Preamble and Text of Amendments 1-10 taken from:
http://www.archives.gov/exhibits/charters/bill_of_rights_transcript.html
Retrieved August 3, 2011

Amendment 6

In all criminal cases, the accused person has the right to a speedy and public trial by an impartial jury from the State and district where the crime was committed. This district must have been previously determined by law. The accused person also has the right to be told exactly what the accusations are about, to confront the witnesses against him or her, to require witnesses in his or her favor to testify, and to have the assistance of a lawyer for his or her defense.

Amendment 7

In lawsuits under common law,[63] where the disputed amount is more than twenty dollars, the right of trial by jury will be preserved. No fact that has been tried by a jury, may be re-examined in any Court of the United States, except according to the rules of the common law.

Amendment 8

Excessive bail may not be required. Excessive fines may not be imposed. Cruel and unusual punishments may not be inflicted.

Amendment 9

The fact that certain rights of the people are listed in the Constitution does not mean that their other rights may be denied, or treated as less important.[64]

Amendment 10

The powers that are not delegated to the United States by the Constitution are retained by the separate States, or by the people. There are exceptions for certain powers that the Constitution prohibits to the States.[65]

AMENDMENT XI *Passed by Congress March 4, 1794. Ratified February 7, 1795.* **Note:** *Article III, section 2, of the Constitution was modified by Amendment 11.*

The Judicial power of the United States shall not be construed to extend to any suit in law or equity, commenced or prosecuted against one of the United States by Citizens of another State, or by Citizens or Subjects of any Foreign State.

AMENDMENT XII *Passed by Congress December 9, 1803. Ratified June 15, 1804.* **Note:** *A portion of Article II, section 1 of the Constitution was superseded by the 12th Amendment.*

The Electors shall meet in their respective states and vote by ballot for President and Vice-President, one of whom, at least, shall not be an inhabitant of the same state with themselves;

they shall name in their ballots the person voted for as President, and in distinct ballots the person voted for as Vice-President, and they shall make distinct lists of all persons voted for as President, and of all persons voted for as Vice-President, and of the number of votes for each, which lists they shall sign and certify, and transmit sealed to the seat of the government of the United States, directed to the President of the Senate;

-- the President of the Senate shall, in the presence of the Senate and House of Representatives, open all the certificates and the votes shall then be counted; -- The person having the greatest number of votes for President, shall be the President, if such number be a majority of the whole number of Electors appointed;

and if no person have such majority, then from the persons having the highest numbers not exceeding three on the list of those voted for as President, the House of Representatives shall choose immediately, by ballot, the President. But in choosing the President, the votes shall be taken by states, the representation from each state having one vote; a quorum for this purpose shall consist of a member or members from two-thirds of the states, and a majority of all the states shall be necessary to a choice.

The Constitution Made Easy

Amendments 11-27

Amendment 11[66]

The judicial power of the United States will not include any kind of suit that is brought against one of the United States by citizens of any other State, or by citizens or subjects of any foreign State.

Amendment 12[67]

Section 1
The electors must meet in their respective States, and vote by ballot for President and Vice President. They may not vote for a President and a Vice President who are both from the same State as the electors.

Section 2
They must name in one set of ballots the person they voted for as President, and in a different set of ballots the person they voted for as Vice President. They must make separate lists of all the persons they voted for as President, and of all persons they voted for as Vice President, and the number of votes for each. They must sign these lists, and certify that they are correct, and send them sealed to the President of the Senate.

Section 3
The President of the Senate must open all the certificates in the presence of the Senate and House of Representatives, and the votes must then be counted. The person receiving the greatest number of votes for President will become the President, as long as he or she receives a majority of the total number of electors.

Section 4
If no person receives a majority, then the House of Representatives must immediately elect the President by ballot. They must choose him or her from the three persons with the highest numbers of votes. In choosing the President, the votes must be taken by States, and each State will have one vote. A quorum for this purpose will consist of at least one member from two-thirds of the States, and a majority of all the States will be necessary for the election to be final.

And if the House of Representatives shall not choose a President whenever the right of choice shall devolve upon them, before the fourth day of March next following, then the Vice-President shall act as President, as in case of the death or other constitutional disability of the President. – [Superseded by Section 3 of the 20th Amendment.]

[See Section 3 of the 20th Amendment]

The person having the greatest number of votes as Vice-President, shall be the Vice-President, if such number be a majority of the whole number of Electors appointed, and if no person have a majority, then from the two highest numbers on the list, the Senate shall choose the Vice-President; a quorum for the purpose shall consist of two-thirds of the whole number of Senators, and a majority of the whole number shall be necessary to a choice. But no person constitutionally ineligible to the office of President shall be eligible to that of Vice-President of the United States.

AMENDMENT XIII *Passed by Congress January 31, 1865. Ratified December 6, 1865. **Note**: A portion of Article IV, section 2, of the Constitution was superseded by the 13th amendment.*

Section 1.
Neither slavery nor involuntary servitude, except as a punishment for crime whereof the party shall have been duly convicted, shall exist within the United States, or any place subject to their jurisdiction.

Section 2.
Congress shall have power to enforce this article by appropriate legislation.

The Constitution Made Easy

Section 5[68]

If the President elect dies before the beginning of his or her term (Noon, January 20th), then the Vice President elect will become President. If a President has not been chosen before the beginning of his or her term, or if the President elect does not qualify, then the Vice President elect will act as President until a qualified President is chosen. [From A:20.3.1]

Section 6

In case neither a President elect, nor a Vice President elect qualifies, Congress may provide for this by law. Then this law will determine who will act as President, or the way in which the Acting President will be selected. This person will act as President until a qualified President or Vice President is chosen. [From A:20.3.2]

Section 7

The person receiving the greatest number of votes for Vice President will become the Vice President, as long as he or she receives a majority of the total number of electors. If no person receives a majority, then the Senate must choose the Vice President from the two persons with the highest numbers of votes. A quorum for this purpose will consist of two-thirds of the total number of Senators, and a majority of the total number will be necessary for the election to be final. If a person is not eligible, under the Constitution, to be President of the United States, that person will not be eligible to be Vice President either.

Amendment 13[69]

Section 1

Slavery and all other forms of involuntary service are forbidden within the United States, and all places under their authority, unless it is punishment for a crime for which the person has been properly convicted.

Section 2

Congress will have power to enforce this Amendment by appropriate laws.

AMENDMENT XIV *Passed by Congress June 13, 1866. Ratified July 9, 1868.* **Note**: *Article I, section 2, of the Constitution was modified by section 2 of the 14th amendment.*

Section 1.

All persons born or naturalized in the United States, and subject to the jurisdiction thereof, are citizens of the United States and of the State wherein they reside. No State shall make or enforce any law which shall abridge the privileges or immunities of citizens of the United States; nor shall any State deprive any person of life, liberty, or property, without due process of law; nor deny to any person within its jurisdiction the equal protection of the laws.

Section 2.

Representatives shall be apportioned among the several States according to their respective numbers, counting the whole number of persons in each State, excluding Indians not taxed. But when the right to vote at any election for the choice of electors for President and Vice-President of the United States, Representatives in Congress, the Executive and Judicial officers of a State, or the members of the Legislature thereof, is denied to any of the male inhabitants of such State, being twenty-one years of age, and citizens of the United States, or in any way abridged, except for participation in rebellion, or other crime, the basis of representation therein shall be reduced in the proportion which the number of such male citizens shall bear to the whole number of male citizens twenty-one years of age in such State. [Changed by the 19th and 26th Amendments.]

Section 3.

No person shall be a Senator or Representative in Congress, or elector of President and Vice-President, or hold any office, civil or military, under the United States, or under any State, who, having previously taken an oath, as a member of Congress, or as an officer of the United States, or as a member of any State legislature, or as an executive or judicial officer of any State, to support the Constitution of the United States, shall have engaged in insurrection or rebellion against the same, or given aid or comfort to the enemies thereof. But Congress may by a vote of two-thirds of each House, remove such disability.

Amendment 14[70]

Section 1

All people who are born or naturalized in the United States, and subject to their authority, are citizens of the United States and of the State they live in. No State may make or enforce any law which diminishes the privileges or freedoms of citizens of the United States. No State may take away any person's life, liberty, or property without proper operation of law. No State may deny any person under its authority the equal protection of the laws.

Section 2

The number of Representatives that each State has will be based upon the population of each State. For these purposes the population will count everybody except Indians who are not taxpayers. The right to vote may not be denied to any citizen in any State who is at least 18 years old.[71] This includes the right to vote for President and Vice President of the United States,[72] Representatives in Congress, as well as the Governor, judges and legislators of that State. If any State prevents or hinders any eligible citizen from voting, unless they participated in rebellion or other crime, the number of Representatives that State is entitled to will be reduced in proportion.

Section 3

Certain people are disqualified from being Senators or Representatives in Congress, or electors of President and Vice President, or holding any official position under the United States, or under any State.[73]

If they were ever a member of Congress, or a member of a State legislature, or an officer of the United States, or an official in any State; and took an oath to support the Constitution of the United States, and then they participated in revolution or rebellion against the Constitution, or if they gave assistance or support to its enemies, then they are disqualified. But Congress may make exceptions by a two-thirds vote of each House.

Section 4.

The validity of the public debt of the United States, authorized by law, including debts incurred for payment of pensions and bounties for services in suppressing insurrection or rebellion, shall not be questioned.

But neither the United States nor any State shall assume or pay any debt or obligation incurred in aid of insurrection or rebellion against the United States, or any claim for the loss or emancipation of any slave; but all such debts, obligations and claims shall be held illegal and void.

Section 5.

The Congress shall have the power to enforce, by appropriate legislation, the provisions of this article.

AMENDMENT XV *Passed by Congress February 26, 1869. Ratified February 3, 1870.*

Section 1.

The right of citizens of the United States to vote shall not be denied or abridged by the United States or by any State on account of race, color, or previous condition of servitude —

Section 2.

The Congress shall have the power to enforce this article by appropriate legislation.

AMENDMENT XVI *Passed by Congress July 2, 1909. Ratified February 3, 1913.* **Note:** *Article I, section 9, of the Constitution was modified by Amendment 16.*

The Congress shall have power to lay and collect taxes on incomes, from whatever source derived, without apportionment among the several States, and without regard to any census or enumeration.

AMENDMENT XVII *Passed by Congress May 13, 1912. Ratified April 8, 1913.* **Note:** *Article I, section 3, of the Constitution was modified by the 17th Amendment.*

The Senate of the United States shall be composed of two Senators from each State, elected by the people thereof, for six years; and each Senator shall have one vote. The electors in each State shall have the qualifications requisite for electors of the most numerous branch of the State legislatures.

The Constitution Made Easy

Section 4

The public debt of the United States is valid and may not be questioned if the debt was authorized by law. These debts include payment of pensions, and rewards for services used in suppressing revolution or rebellion.

But neither the United States, nor any State, may assume or pay any debt or obligation incurred as part of any revolution or rebellion against the United States. They may not pay any claim for the loss or freeing of any slave. All such debts, obligations and claims will be regarded as illegal and void.[74]

Section 5

Congress will have power to enforce the provisions of this Amendment by appropriate laws.

Amendment 15[75]

Section 1

The right of citizens of the United States to vote shall not be denied or diminished by the United States, or by any State, because of race, color, or previously being a slave.

Section 2

Congress will have power to enforce this Amendment by appropriate laws.

Amendment 16[76]

Congress will have power to assess and collect taxes on income from all sources. These taxes will not be based on the census, or divided proportionately between the States.

Amendment 17[77]

Section 1

The Senate of the United States will consist of two Senators from each State, elected by the people of that State, for six years; and each Senator will have one vote. Each State has a standard it uses to decide who is allowed to vote for its own State legislature. This same standard must be used to determine who is allowed to vote for members of the Senate.

When vacancies happen in the representation of any State in the Senate, the executive authority of such State shall issue writs of election to fill such vacancies: *Provided*, That the legislature of any State may empower the executive thereof to make temporary appointments until the people fill the vacancies by election as the legislature may direct.

This amendment shall not be so construed as to affect the election or term of any Senator chosen before it becomes valid as part of the Constitution.

AMENDMENT XVIII *Passed by Congress December 18, 1917. Ratified January 16, 1919. Repealed by Amendment 21.*

Section 1.
After one year from the ratification of this article the manufacture, sale, or transportation of intoxicating liquors within, the importation thereof into, or the exportation thereof from the United States and all territory subject to the jurisdiction thereof for beverage purposes is hereby prohibited.

Section 2.
The Congress and the several States shall have concurrent power to enforce this article by appropriate legislation.

Section 3.
This article shall be inoperative unless it shall have been ratified as an amendment to the Constitution by the legislatures of the several States, as provided in the Constitution, within seven years from the date of the submission hereof to the States by the Congress.

AMENDMENT XIX *Passed by Congress June 4, 1919. Ratified August 18, 1920.*
The right of citizens of the United States to vote shall not be denied or abridged by the United States or by any State on account of sex.

Congress shall have power to enforce this article by appropriate legislation.

Section 2

When any Senator does not finish his or her term, the Governor from his or her State must set a Special Election to fill the remainder of that term. However, the legislature of that State may give the Governor power to make a temporary appointment that will only last until the position is filled by the Special Election.

Section 3

This Amendment may not be interpreted in a way that affects the election or term of any Senator who has already been elected when this Amendment becomes part of the Constitution.

Amendment 18

Section 1

One year after this Amendment receives final approval, it will be illegal to manufacture, sell, or transport alcoholic beverages within the United States, and United States territories. It will also be illegal to import or export alcoholic beverages into, or out of, the United States and United States territories. [Replaced by the 21[78]st Amendment]

Section 2

Congress and the separate States will all have power to make laws that enforce this Amendment.

Section 3

This Amendment will not go into effect unless it is approved by the legislatures of the various States, as described in the Constitution. The final approval process must also be completed within seven years from the date Congress sends it to the States.

Amendment 19[79]

Section 1

The right of citizens of the United States to vote shall not be denied or diminished by the United States, or by any State, because of gender.

Section 2

Congress will have power to enforce this Amendment by appropriate laws.

The Constitution of the United States

AMENDMENT XX *Passed by Congress March 2, 1932. Ratified January 23, 1933. **Note:** Article I, section 4, of the Constitution was modified by section 2 of this amendment. In addition, a portion of the 12th amendment was superseded by section 3.*

Section 1.

The terms of the President and the Vice President shall end at noon on the 20th day of January, and the terms of Senators and Representatives at noon on the 3d day of January, of the years in which such terms would have ended if this article had not been ratified; and the terms of their successors shall then begin.

Section 2.

The Congress shall assemble at least once in every year, and such meeting shall begin at noon on the 3d day of January, unless they shall by law appoint a different day.

Section 3.

If, at the time fixed for the beginning of the term of the President, the President elect shall have died, the Vice President elect shall become President. If a President shall not have been chosen before the time fixed for the beginning of his term, or if the President elect shall have failed to qualify, then the Vice President elect shall act as President until a President shall have qualified;

and the Congress may by law provide for the case wherein neither a President elect nor a Vice President shall have qualified, declaring who shall then act as President, or the manner in which one who is to act shall be selected, and such person shall act accordingly until a President or Vice President shall have qualified.

Section 4.

The Congress may by law provide for the case of the death of any of the persons from whom the House of Representatives may choose a President whenever the right of choice shall have devolved upon them, and for the case of the death of any of the persons from whom the Senate may choose a Vice President whenever the right of choice shall have devolved upon them.

Amendment 20

Section 1[80]

The terms of the President and the Vice President will end at Noon on January 20th. The terms of Senators and Representatives will end at Noon on January 3rd. The terms of their successors will then begin. The years in which these various terms end, and others begin, is not changed by this Amendment.

Section 2[81]

Congress must meet at least once in every year, and the meeting will begin at Noon on January 3rd, unless the date is changed by Law.

Section 3[82]

20.3.1 If the President elect dies before the beginning of his or her term (Noon, January 20th), then the Vice President elect will become President. If a President has not been chosen before the beginning of his or her term, or if the President elect does not qualify, then the Vice President elect will act as President until a qualified President is chosen.

20.3.2 In case neither a President elect, nor a Vice President elect qualifies, Congress may provide for this by law. Then this law will determine who will act as President, or the way in which the Acting President will be selected. This person will act as President until a qualified President or Vice President is chosen.

Section 4

The right to choose the President may end up with the House of Representatives (see Amendment 12, Section 4). The right to choose the Vice President may end up with the Senate (see Amendment 12, Section 7). In either case, it is possible that one of the candidates could die before the House or Senate could vote. Congress may write a law to provide for this possibility.

Section 5.

Sections 1 and 2 shall take effect on the 15th day of October following the ratification of this article.

Section 6.

This article shall be inoperative unless it shall have been ratified as an amendment to the Constitution by the legislatures of three-fourths of the several States within seven years from the date of its submission.

AMENDMENT XXI *Passed by Congress February 20, 1933. Ratified December 5, 1933.*

Section 1.

The eighteenth article of amendment to the Constitution of the United States is hereby repealed.

Section 2.

The transportation or importation into any State, Territory, or Possession of the United States for delivery or use therein of intoxicating liquors, in violation of the laws thereof, is hereby prohibited.

Section 3.

This article shall be inoperative unless it shall have been ratified as an amendment to the Constitution by conventions in the several States, as provided in the Constitution, within seven years from the date of the submission hereof to the States by the Congress.

AMENDMENT XXII *Passed by Congress March 21, 1947. Ratified February 27, 1951.*

Section 1.

No person shall be elected to the office of the President more than twice, and no person who has held the office of President, or acted as President, for more than two years of a term to which some other person was elected President shall be elected to the office of President more than once. But this Article shall not apply to any person holding the office of President when this Article was proposed by Congress, and shall not prevent any person who may be holding the office of President, or acting as President, during the term within which this Article becomes operative from holding the office of President or acting as President during the remainder of such term.

The Constitution Made Easy

Section 5
     Sections 1 and 2 shall take effect on the October 15th following the final approval of this Amendment.

Section 6
     This Amendment will not go into effect unless it is approved by the legislatures of three-fourths of the States. The final approval process must also be completed within seven years from the date Congress sends it to the States.

Amendment 21

Section 1
     This Amendment repeals (cancels out) the 18th Amendment of the Constitution.

Section 2
     Alcoholic beverages may not be transported or imported into any State, Territory or Possession of the United States if it violates their laws, and if these beverages are going to be delivered or consumed there.

Section 3
     This Amendment will not go into effect unless it is approved by the legislatures of the various States, as described in the Constitution. The final approval process must also be completed within seven years from the date Congress sends it to the States.

Amendment 22[83]

Section 1
     No person may be elected to the office of President more than twice. If a person has already served as President or Acting President for more than two years of someone else's term, they may only be elected once. This Amendment will not apply to the person who is President or Acting President when this Amendment was proposed by Congress. If this Amendment is approved and becomes effective, it will not prevent the person who is President or Acting President at that time from finishing his or her term.

Section 2.

This article shall be inoperative unless it shall have been ratified as an amendment to the Constitution by the legislatures of three-fourths of the several States within seven years from the date of its submission to the States by the Congress.

AMENDMENT XXIII *Passed by Congress June 16, 1960. Ratified March 29, 1961.*

Section 1.

The District constituting the seat of Government of the United States shall appoint in such manner as Congress may direct: A number of electors of President and Vice President equal to the whole number of Senators and Representatives in Congress to which the District would be entitled if it were a State, but in no event more than the least populous State; they shall be in addition to those appointed by the States, but they shall be considered, for the purposes of the election of President and Vice President, to be electors appointed by a State; and they shall meet in the District and perform such duties as provided by the twelfth article of amendment.

Section 2.

The Congress shall have power to enforce this article by appropriate legislation.

AMENDMENT XXIV *Passed by Congress August 27, 1962. Ratified January 23, 1964.*

Section 1.

The right of citizens of the United States to vote in any primary or other election for President or Vice President, for electors for President or Vice President, or for Senator or Representative in Congress, shall not be denied or abridged by the United States or any State by reason of failure to pay poll tax or other tax.

Section 2.

The Congress shall have power to enforce this article by appropriate legislation.

The Constitution Made Easy

Section 2

This Amendment will not go into effect unless it is approved by the legislatures of three-fourths of the States. The final approval process must also be completed within seven years from the date Congress sends it to the States.

Amendment 23[84]

Section 1

Washington, D.C.[85] may appoint electors for President and Vice President in the way that Congress decides. The number of electors will be calculated as if this District was the State with the least population. These electors will be in addition to the ones appointed by the States, but they shall be treated the same as if they were appointed by a State for this purpose. They shall meet in the District and perform the same duties that are required of States by the 12th Amendment.

Section 2

Congress will have power to enforce this Amendment by appropriate laws.

Amendment 24[86]

Section 1

The right of citizens of the United States to vote shall not be denied or diminished by the United States, or by any State, for failure to pay a poll tax, or other tax. This right includes voting in primary elections, and other elections. It includes voting for President and Vice President,[87] and voting for Senators and Representatives in Congress.

Section 2

Congress will have power to enforce this Amendment by appropriate laws.

The Constitution of the United States

AMENDMENT XXV *Passed by Congress July 6, 1965. Ratified February 10, 1967.* **Note:** *Article II, section 1, of the Constitution was affected by the 25th amendment.*

Section 1.

In case of the removal of the President from office or of his death or resignation, the Vice President shall become President.

Section 2.

Whenever there is a vacancy in the office of the Vice President, the President shall nominate a Vice President who shall take office upon confirmation by a majority vote of both Houses of Congress.

Section 3.

Whenever the President transmits to the President pro tempore of the Senate and the Speaker of the House of Representatives his written declaration that he is unable to discharge the powers and duties of his office, and until he transmits to them a written declaration to the contrary, such powers and duties shall be discharged by the Vice President as Acting President.

Section 4.

Whenever the Vice President and a majority of either the principal officers of the executive departments or of such other body as Congress may by law provide, transmit to the President pro tempore of the Senate and the Speaker of the House of Representatives their written declaration that the President is unable to discharge the powers and duties of his office, the Vice President shall immediately assume the powers and duties of the office as Acting President.

Thereafter, when the President transmits to the President pro tempore of the Senate and the Speaker of the House of Representatives his written declaration that no inability exists, he shall resume the powers and duties of his office unless the Vice President and a majority of either the principal officers of the executive department or of such other body as Congress may by law provide, transmit within four days to the President pro tempore of the Senate and the Speaker of the House of Representatives their written declaration that the President is unable to discharge the powers and duties of his office.

Amendment 25[88]

Section 1
In case of the removal of the President from office, or of his or her death or resignation, the Vice President will become President.

Section 2
Whenever there is a vacancy in the office of the Vice President, the President must nominate a new Vice President. He will take office upon confirmation by a majority vote of both Houses of Congress.

Section 3
Whenever the President believes that he or she is unable to carry out the powers and duties of office, he or she may send written declaration to the temporary President of the Senate and to the Speaker of the House of Representatives. Until the President sends them a written declaration that he or she has become able again, these powers and duties must be discharged by the Vice President as Acting President.

Section 4
Whenever the Vice President and a majority of the Cabinet officers[89] agree that the President is unable to discharge the powers and duties of office, they may send their written declaration to the temporary President of the Senate and the Speaker of the House of Representatives. Then the Vice President must immediately assume the powers and duties as Acting President. (Congress may change this in the future from "the Cabinet" to some other group they designate by law.)

Section 5
After this, if the President believes that no inability exists, he or she must send written declaration to the temporary President of the Senate and to the Speaker of the House of Representatives. The President will resume the powers and duties of office unless the Vice President and a majority of the Cabinet officers oppose him or her. If they do, they must send their written declaration within four days to the temporary President of the Senate and to the Speaker of the House of Representatives reasserting that the President is unable to discharge the powers and duties of office.

Thereupon Congress shall decide the issue, assembling within forty-eight hours for that purpose if not in session. If the Congress, within twenty-one days after receipt of the latter written declaration, or, if Congress is not in session, within twenty-one days after Congress is required to assemble, determines by two-thirds vote of both Houses that the President is unable to discharge the powers and duties of his office, the Vice President shall continue to discharge the same as Acting President; otherwise, the President shall resume the powers and duties of his office.

AMENDMENT XXVI *Passed by Congress March 23, 1971. Ratified July 1, 1971.* **Note:** *Amendment 14, section 2, of the Constitution was modified by section 1 of the 26th amendment.*

Section 1.
The right of citizens of the United States, who are eighteen years of age or older, to vote shall not be denied or abridged by the United States or by any State on account of age.

Section 2.
The Congress shall have power to enforce this article by appropriate legislation.

AMENDMENT XXVII *Originally proposed Sept. 25, 1789. Ratified May 7, 1992.*

No law, varying the compensation for the services of the Senators and Representatives, shall take effect, until an election of representatives shall have intervened.

Text of Amendments 11-27 taken from:
http://www.archives.gov/exhibits/charters/constitution_amendments_11-27.html -- Retrieved August 3, 2011

The Constitution Made Easy

Section 6

At this point Congress must decide the issue. They must meet within 48 hours for this purpose if they are not already in session. Congress must make a determination within 21 days of receiving the most recent declaration (or 23 days if they were not in session). If Congress determines that the President is unable to discharge the powers and duties of office, then the Vice President will continue as Acting President. They must do this by two-thirds vote of both Houses. Otherwise, the President will resume the powers and duties of his or her office.

Amendment 26[90]

Section 1

The right of citizens of the United States to vote shall not be denied or diminished by the United States, or by any State, because of age, as long as they are eighteen years of age or older.

Section 2

Congress will have power to enforce this Amendment by appropriate laws.

Amendment 27[91]

No law that changes the pay of Senators and Representatives will take effect until after the next election of Representatives has taken place.

---

[1] This is known as the "Elector (voter) Qualification Clause." The original says, "for the most numerous Branch of the State Legislature." At the time it was possible that voting requirements could be different from one branch to the other. But as modified by various amendments, almost anyone over 18 years of age can now vote in virtually any election. See **C:1.2.3**, and the several amendments that affect it.

[2] *Legislature* means any "group of law-makers." In the Constitution, the term refers consistently to the law-makers of one or more of the States; *not* to Congress. Congress is first mentioned by saying it will have "all *legislative* Powers herein granted" (**C:1.1.1**). But after that introduction, they are consistently called *Congress*, or when just one House is in view, the *House of Representatives*, or the *Senate*. The Constitution frequently refers to Congress's power to *make law*, but never calls them a *legislature*.

[3] Every reference to *he, him, his,* etc. has been changed to gender-neutral or gender-inclusive terminology to show the effect of the 19th Amendment which gave women the right to vote in 1920.

[4] This Clause was superseded by Section 2 of the 14th Amendment, which has replaced nearly all of it here except for a few words concerning taxes, which the 14th Amendment did not address. The original text counted three-fifths of the slave population for both representation and taxation. This was known as the *three-fifths compromise*. In 1868, the 14th Amendment voided this formula, and added language about the right to vote. Several other amendments expanded this right.

[5] Under the original Constitution, all *direct taxes* had to be calculated in such a way that the amount each State paid was in proportion to its population (*apportioned*) (**C:1.9.4**). The 16th Amendment created an exception. See Amendment 16 and endnote.

[6] This sentence incorporates the effects of the 15th, 19th, 24th and 26th Amendments concerning race, gender, poll tax, and age.

[7] When voters cast their ballots for President and Vice President, they are actually choosing *electors* from their State (or from Washington, D.C.). These electors in turn vote for President and Vice President, as described in **C:2.1**.

[8] Congress determines the number of Representatives, provided that each State must have at least one, the number must be proportional to population, and there may not be more than one for every thirty thousand people. The number of Representatives rose steadily until 1911, when it was fixed at 435 where it remains today. Nothing in the Constitution prevents Congress from changing the number in the future.

[9] An *Impeachment* is a formal *charge* of wrongdoing that can only be brought by the House of Representatives, as indicated here. The actual trial to determine *guilt* takes place in the Senate (**C:1.3.7-8**).

[10] This paragraph is the text of **A:17.1**, which changed the method of electing Senators and added the qualifications of voters to be the same as for

Representatives. Prior to approval of the 17th Amendment in 1913, the Constitution required Senators to be chosen by their respective State legislatures.

[11] The original says, "for the most numerous Branch of the State Legislature." See **C:1.2.1** and endnote.

[12] This paragraph is the text of **A:17.2**, which modified the provisions for filling vacancies.

[13] The person who *presides* over something, whether it is a corporation, college, bank or government, is called the *President* of that entity. In the Constitution, *President* refers to the chief executive of the United States (see Article 2). The person who would take over his duties if he died, or became unable to continue in office, is called the *Vice President*. If the Vice President takes over, even temporarily, during that time he is called the *Acting President*. The Vice President is also the *President* of the Senate. He *presides* over it much of the time. When he is not there, the *President pro tempore* presides. The *President elect* and *Vice President elect* have been elected, but have not yet had their terms begin or taken their oaths of office. See 1.4.2 and Amendment 20 and the endnotes for more information on the time between elections and the beginnings of terms.

[14] The original phrase here is *pro tempore,* which means *temporary*, or *for the time*.

[15] According to Webster's 1828 Dictionary *Preside* means, "To be set over for the exercise of authority; to direct, control and govern, as the chief officer. A man may *preside* over a nation or province; or he may *preside* over a senate, or a meeting of citizens."

[16] An *Impeachment* is a formal *charge* of wrongdoing that can only be brought by the House of Representatives (**C:1.2.6**). The actual trial to determine *guilt* takes place in the Senate, as indicated here.

[17] The original says, "they shall be on Oath or Affirmation." Before conducting an impeachment trial, the Senators take an oath to act impartially as if they were judges or jurors. Generally, people who object to taking an oath in any court (often on religious grounds), may instead *affirm* that they will act impartially, or tell the truth, or whatever would have been expected if they had taken an oath.

[18] For example, an official could be *impeached* if he or she was accused of murder (or some other serious crime). If the House of Representatives *impeached* that official, and the Senate *convicted* him or her, the most they could do is remove the official from office, and ban him or her from future office. That would not let the official off the hook for the murder (or the other serious crime). He or she could, and most likely would, be arrested and tried by the proper authorities.

[19] The original adds an exception for the *place* of choosing Senators. At the time, Senators were chosen by State Legislatures, so it was important for States to retain autonomy over the *place* of those elections. The 17th Amendment changed the method of electing Senators to a popular election. There is no mention in the 17th Amendment of where the elections take place, or who has

final authority to decide this, but it is likely a moot point and so it was left out of this version.

[20] Some of this language is from the 20th Amendment which took effect in 1933. Until then, the date that the *terms* of Congress began and ended were simply set by law, not by the Constitution. For more information, see the 20th Amendment, Sections 1 and 2, and the endnotes.

[21] A *quorum* is the minimum number of persons that must be present for a group to conduct business. Often, as here, a majority is considered a *quorum*. But it can be a different number (**C:2.1.6** and **2.1.9**).

[22] *Adjourn* means to end a meeting, usually with a plan to reconvene at a later time, and/or in another place.

[23] The language about the change in pay is from the 27th Amendment (1992), and is included here.

[24] Courts have held that this protection generally extends only to civil arrests (which are virtually non-existent today), not criminal arrests. This portion of the Clause may be obsolete for all practical purposes.

[25] The original says "*general Welfare.*" The meaning here has to do with the mutual well-being of all the member States. This can be seen more clearly in the Articles of Confederation ("[the States] mutual and general welfare…", "for the defense and welfare of the United States, or any of them…"). Webster's 1828 Dictionary defines *Welfare* as, "Exemption from any unusual evil or calamity; the enjoyment of peace and prosperity, or the ordinary blessings of society and civil government; applied to states."

[26] These kinds of taxes were considered *indirect*. The Constitutional standard for *indirect taxes* was that they be *uniform* or consistent, the same everywhere. Contrast this with *direct taxes* which had to be *apportioned,* or in proportion to population (**C:1.9.4**).The 16th Amendment allowed Congress to assess an income tax, which is a *direct tax* that is *not based* upon population. Until this Amendment was ratified in 1913, all *direct taxes* were required to be *apportioned* (**C:1.9.4**). Income tax also affected **C:1.2.3**. The effect has been incorporated into those texts.

[27] Section 1 of the 14th Amendment expanded this Power by defining citizenship and adding federal protection for the rights of citizens.

[28] In the original, these letters of retaliation were called *Letters of Marque and Reprisal.* These letters were given by various governments to permit private citizens to do a number of things normally associated with the military. They could recover lost property, or use force to get even with the enemy for damages. They were sometimes authorized to capture enemies and enemy ships.

[29] *Captures* probably means *property* that was captured. But there is some evidence that the meaning might also include captured *people*, so it was not modernized, as any synonym might prejudice the meaning.

[30] There is much discussion about the meaning of the term *Militia* as it has evolved over the years. But at the time that the Constitution was drafted and ratified, nearly all able-bodied men in any State were considered to be part of

that State's Militia. They were expected to keep their own *arms*, and bring those arms with them to fight when needed, as they had just done during the Revolution. See also the 2nd Amendment and endnote.

[31] The original doesn't mention Washington, D.C. since that District had not yet been selected. Washington, D.C. (District of Columbia) has been "the Seat of the Government of the United States" since 1800. See also Amendment 23 and endnote.

[32] These are storage areas around a dock, especially for naval supplies.

[33] This Section includes limits on taxing, law-making and the United States Government in general. It also lists certain rights of citizens and State protections. There are substantial parallels to the Bill of Rights which expand on the same concepts.

[34] This was an oblique reference to the slave trade which was protected by this compromise for about twenty years. At the first Constitutionally-permitted opportunity, a federal law banning all future slave trade was passed by Congress and signed by President Thomas Jefferson. It became effective on January 1, 1808. Slavery itself was abolished by the 13th Amendment in 1865. The whole Clause may be obsolete, but it was retained here because it was changed by Law; not repealed or replaced by Amendment. Some State authority regarding immigration in general may remain.

[35] This right to be seen by a judge to determine whether a person is being properly held is called a *Writ of Habeas Corpus*.

[36] This kind of law was called a *Bill of Attainder*. It was an act of a legislature that found a person guilty, usually of treason. These bills have a very complex history, including putting people to death and then confiscating their property. Under the Constitution, Congress can set the penalty for treason (**C:3.3.2**), but guilt is determined by courts.

[37] These kinds of laws were called *ex post facto Laws*. That is the term used in the original. It means *after the fact*. So Congress may not decide that something *should have been* a crime, and make a law that goes backwards in time to punish the person(s) who did it.

[38] The Constitutional standard for *direct taxes* is that they be *apportioned*, meaning shared in proportion to each State's population. The income tax (allowed by the 16th Amendment in 1913) became the exception to that rule. See Amendment 16 and endnote.

[39] Many other countries at the time, including England, had *classes* of people. There were *nobles* of various ranks, such as duke, marquis, earl, viscount and baron. These people were regarded as having a higher rank in society than the rest, called *commoners*.

[40] Section 1 of the 14th Amendment contains additional prohibitions concerning what States may not do.

[41] *Letters of Marque and Reprisal*. See **C:1.8.11** and the endnote.

[42] *Bills of Attainder*. See **C:1.9.3** and the endnote.

[43] *Ex post facto Laws*. See **C:1.9.3** and the endnote.

[44] The original does not set any limit on the number of terms a President may serve. Since 1951, the 22nd Amendment has limited Presidents to being *elected* to two terms. It also allows for them to have previously served up to two years of someone else's term. See the 22nd Amendment for more detail.

[45] The original does not establish the beginning and ending of the President's term. This was simply set by law as March 4th until 1933 when the 20th Amendment changed it to January 20th, and made it part of the Constitution. Federal election dates are still set by law, and are presently the Tuesday after the first Monday in November in even-numbered years. A President is elected in every other Federal election, so if a year is divisible by four, there will be a Presidential election that year in November. The President will take office at Noon on January 20th of the following year.

[46] Originally, only the States appointed electors. In 1961, the 23rd Amendment gave Washington, D.C. the right to appoint some electors. For details, see **A:23**, and the endnote.

[47] The next seven Clauses are the full text of the 12th Amendment which superseded the original. The addition of these Clauses lengthens this section considerably over the original, and changes the numbering of the Clauses significantly. The method of electing the President was changed in 1804 by the 12th Amendment and again in 1933 by the 20th Amendment. Clauses **2.1.3** through **2.1.9** are the full text of the 12th Amendment, *as amended by* the 20th Amendment. So there are actually two paragraphs that appear in this Version three times: **A:20.3.1-2** became **A:12.5-6**, which became **C:2.1.7-8**.

[48] **C:2.1.12-13**, and **15-18** are the text of the 25th Amendment (1967). They supersede one simple paragraph in the original text about Presidential succession. The addition of these Clauses lengthens this Section considerably over the original, and changes the numbering of the Clauses significantly.

[49] This provision allows Congress to write laws that determine who will be President if *both* the President and Vice President become unable to serve for any reason. The law that currently determines this is called the Presidential Succession Act of 1947 (as amended). Under this law, the Speaker of the House of Representatives is next in line behind the Vice President. Then follows the President pro tempore of the Senate, the Secretary of State and the other members of the Cabinet.

[50] The actual language says "a majority of... the principal officers of the executive departments." These department heads are often referred to as the President's Cabinet or Cabinet officers.

[51] Two provisions in this Clause were nullified in 1795 by the 11th Amendment, and so they have been deleted here. Before the 11th Amendment, the Supreme Court also had authority over controversies between one State and citizens of a different State; and also between a State (or its citizens), and a foreign State (or its citizens).

[52] The original uses the phrase, *work corruption of blood.* Under *common law* (see Amendment 7 and the endnote), traitors would be executed and their

property would then be confiscated. This also had the effect of punishing the traitor's heirs, or bloodline.

[53] *General Laws* would be uniform from State to State, not specific to a certain case.

[54] The original had a Clause about returning slaves who escaped. This was nullified by the 13th Amendment in 1865, so that Clause is deleted here.

[55] In this paragraph various forms of the word "approve," replace various forms of the word "ratify," which appear in the original.

[56] The *Confederation* was the arrangement the States operated under before this Constitution was ratified (approved) in 1789. The *Articles of Confederation* was the agreement between the States that served much the same function as the Constitution. It was under this agreement that the *Confederacy* actually became known as *The United States of America*. It was drafted by the Second Continental Congress in 1777 and ratified (approved) by all 13 States in 1781, all while fighting the Revolutionary War. The framers of the Constitution met in Philadelphia in 1787 for the purpose of *amending* these *Articles*, and ended up drafting a brand new agreement. Here (**C:6.1**), the framers are reaffirming all debts and agreements made while they were operating under the *Articles of Confederation*.

[57] These first ten Amendments of the Constitution were proposed and ratified (approved) as a group. Some States refused to ratify the Constitution unless this *Bill of Rights* was promised. 12 Amendments were proposed by Congress, and these 10 were ratified effective December 15, 1791. One, concerning Congressional pay raises, was ratified over two hundred years later as the 27th Amendment.

[58] The original uses the term *arms*, which includes other military weapons and armor.

[59] For definition of *Militia*, see **C:1.8.15** and endnote.

[60] The original calls this reasonable belief *probable cause*. Just how *probable* the *cause* has to be for a warrant to be issued has been the subject of many court cases.

[61] The original says *oath* or *affirmation*. People who object to making a statement under oath (often on religious grounds), may instead *affirm* that they are telling the truth.

[62] This sentence only affected serious crimes in 1791. But in modern practice, this principle of "double jeopardy" has been extended by the courts to include all, or nearly all, crimes. This has had the effect of *increasing* the protection guaranteed by this Amendment.

[63] *Common law* is a big subject. But a short definition is that it is the unwritten law that has been universally accepted for a very, very long time.

[64] While some of the founders would not support the Constitution without a Bill of Rights, others opposed it on the grounds that listing a few of their rights, might cause their other rights to be "denied or disparaged." The Ninth Amendment was included to address this concern.

[65] The list of powers that the United States Government *does have* is contained in the Constitution. They are often referred to as *enumerated*, or numbered, powers. Most of them are listed in **C:1.8**. The list of powers the States *do not have* is also contained in the Constitution. Most of these are listed in **C:1.10**.

[66] The effect of the 11th Amendment on **C:3.2** has already been incorporated into the text of that Section.

[67] The 12th Amendment substantially affected **C:2.1**, superseding much of the original language. As a result, the entire Amendment has been duplicated and inserted into this Version as **C:2.1.3** to **2.1.9**.

[68] The next two Sections are actually **A:20.3.1-2** which superseded one sentence in the original.

[69] The effect of the 13th Amendment on **C:4.2.2** has already been incorporated into the text of that Clause. See also **C:1.9.1** and endnote.

[70] Section 1 of the 14th Amendment has the effect of adding new power for the United States to define citizenship and protect the freedoms of citizens (see **C:1.8.4**). It also limits what States may do as listed in **C:1.10**. Section 2 superseded **C:1.2.3**, and has already been duplicated and added there, virtually replacing that Clause except for a few words concerning taxes.

[71] This sentence also incorporates the effects of the 15th, 19th, 24th, and 26th Amendments concerning race, gender, poll tax, and age.

[72] When voters cast their ballots for President and Vice President, they are actually choosing *electors* from their State (or from Washington, D.C.). These electors in turn vote for President and Vice President, as described in **C:2.1**.

[73] This Section was designed to disqualify people who had held certain offices and then participated in the Civil War on the Side of the South.

[74] This Section affirms all debts incurred by the North in the Civil War; but nullifies all debts incurred by the South.

[75] The effect of the 15th Amendment on **A:14.2**, and on **C:1.2.3** has already been incorporated into those texts.

[76] The 16th Amendment had the effect of adding a new Power of Congress like those listed in **C:1.8**. It also affected **C:1.2.3** and **C:1.9.4**. The effect has been incorporated into those texts.

[77] The effects of the 17th Amendment on **C:1.3.1** and **C:1.3.3** have already been incorporated into those texts.

[78] It is often said that the 21st Amendment *repealed,* or cancelled out, the 18th Amendment, and Section 1 of the 21st Amendment says just that. But Section 2 then offers new language that has *Federal* implications for violating *State* laws concerning the transporting and importing of alcoholic beverages.

[79] The effect of the 19th Amendment on **A:14.2**, and on **C:1.2.3** has already been incorporated into those texts.

[80] Section 1 of the 20th Amendment establishes the *terms* for President, Vice President, Senators and Representatives. The effect on the President's term was incorporated into **C:2.1.1**. (The President's term was restated for clarity in Section 3 of this Version.)

[81] Section 2 of the 20th Amendment establishes the first *meeting* date of Congress in each year. Sections 1 and 2 affected **C:1.4.2** and the effects have been incorporated there. Until the 20th Amendment took effect in 1933, the date that the *terms* of Congress and the President began and ended were simply set by law, not by the Constitution. From the beginning, Congress set that date as March 4. The Constitution set the first *meeting* date as "the first Monday in December," so nine months would elapse between the start of the term and the first meeting. A few more months would elapse between Federal *elections* and the start of the *term*. So a full year could elapse between the *elections* and the first *meeting*. Because of the 20th Amendment, there is a much shorter time between Congressional elections and the date their terms begin. Their first meeting is now set for the same day as the start of their term. (The first meeting date, but not the date the term begins, may still be changed by law). Similarly, the President's term now begins on January 20th.

[82] Section 3 of the 20th Amendment superseded Section 5 of the 12th Amendment. The 12th Amendment had already superseded several Clauses in Article 2, Section 1. The 12th Amendment, as amended by the 20th Amendment, is seen again in this Version as **C:2.1.3-9**. See **C:2.1.3-9**, and Amendment 12, and the endnotes.

[83] The effect of this Amendment on **C:2.1.1** has already been incorporated into the text of that Clause.

[84] The effect of this Amendment on **C:2.1.2** has already been incorporated into the text of that Clause.

[85] The original calls Washington, D.C. "the District constituting the seat of Government of the United States." Washington, D.C. (District of Columbia) has been the seat of Government of the United States since 1800.

[86] The effect of this Amendment on **A:14.2**, and on **C:1.2.3** has already been incorporated into those texts.

[87] When voters cast their ballots for President and Vice President, they are actually choosing *electors* from their State (or from Washington, D.C.). These electors in turn vote for President and Vice President, as described in **C:2.1**.

[88] This Amendment substantially affected **C:2.1**, superseding some of the original language. As a result, the entire Amendment has been duplicated and inserted into this version as **C:2.1.12-13, 15-18**.

[89] The actual language says "a majority of... the principal officers of the executive departments." These department heads are often referred to as the President's Cabinet or Cabinet officers.

[90] The effects of this Amendment on **A:14.2** and **C:1.2.3** have already been incorporated into those texts.

[91] This Amendment affected **C:1.6.1**, and the effects have been incorporated. It was proposed as one of the original Bill of Rights, but it was not approved until over two hundred years later, which was possible because there was no deadline set for ratification. Some more recent Amendments have set seven-year deadlines for ratification.

Recommended Resources

Many of these resources are available online and in print. One online resource may be suggested, but there are usually others that can be easily found using any standard search engine.

Blackstone, William, Sir. *Commentaries on the Laws of England*. Oxford: Clarendon Press, 1765-1769. (Note: This version is available online at the Avalon Project of Yale Law School. http://avalon.law.yale.edu/subject_menus/blackstone.asp)

    For the very serious student who wishes to understand the fundamentals of English law that provided much of the legal framework and background that the framers of the Constitution would have been familiar with.

Farrand, Max, ed. *The Records of the Federal Convention of 1787*. New Haven: Yale University Press, 1911. 3 vols. (Note: This version is available at the Online Library of Liberty. http://oll.libertyfund.org/index.php?option=com_staticxt&staticfile=show.php?title=1785&Itemid=27)

    Once again, this is a resource for the serious student because of its size; but anyone can enjoy perusing excerpts. Includes the notes of James Madison which have also been published separately. A later "Supplement" to these records is also available from Yale University Press.

Hamilton, Alexander et al. *The Federalist*. Benjamin Fletcher Wright, ed. New York: Barnes and Noble, 2004. (Note: Another version is available at the Online Library of Liberty. http://oll.libertyfund.org/index.php?option=com_staticxt&staticfile=show.php%3Ftitle=788&Itemid=27)

    This is a standard volume for students of the Constitution. One or more versions are available at most bookstores. Contains the arguments of Alexander Hamilton, James Madison and John Jay as they wrote (under the collective pseudonym of *Publius*) in favor of ratifying the new Constitution.

The Constitution Made Easy -Endnotes

Hirsch, E.D. *Validity in Interpretation*. New Haven: Yale University Press, 1967.
>A standard work on the principles of literary interpretation.

Ketcham, Ralph, ed. *The Anti-Federalist Papers and the Constitutional Convention Debates*. New York: New American Library - Signet Classics, 2003. (Note: Similar information is available online at http://www.constitution.org/afp/afp.htm)
>This collection is reader friendly and includes many of the best portions of the larger compilations by Farrand and Storing.

Meese III, Edwin, ed. *The Heritage Guide to the Constitution*. Washington, DC: Regnery Publishing Company, 2005.
>This is an almost line-by-line commentary on the Constitution from a number of contributors who generally observe the originalist perspective. Relevant court cases are also frequently cited and discussed.

Storing, Herbert J. *The Complete Anti-Federalist*. Chicago: University of Chicago Press, 1981.
>Several American patriots gave speeches and wrote articles opposing the approval of the new Constitution, believing that the *Articles of Confederation* were sufficient for an alliance of independent States. These writers generally wrote under pseudonyms, but included Patrick Henry and other well-known figures of the Revolution. Storing also published an excerpted version in 1985 called simply, *The Anti-Federalist*.

Story, Joseph. *Commentaries on the Constitution of the United States*. Boston: Hilliard, Gray and Company, 1833.
(Note: This version is available online at The Constitution Society. www.constitution.org/js/js_000.htm)

Webster, Noah. *American Dictionary of the English Language 1828*. Reprinted Chesapeake Virginia: FACE Publishing, 1968. (Note: Online word searches available at: http://1828.mshaffer.com/)
>This dictionary was published less than 40 years after the drafting of the Constitution and captures the meaning of the words as they were used at the time more closely than later dictionaries.

Thanks:

The author wishes to thank his family for their help and sacrifice, and for putting up with the long hours involved in this project. To Cat: You have always believed in me, and I owe it all to you. To Denae, Mary, Levi and AmyJoy: Daddy loves you and owes you a special day.

Debts of gratitude are owed to Kirk DouPonce at DogEared Design for an incredible job on the book cover, and Dennis Cheaqui at GD Printing and Graphics for many extra hours typesetting and printing to almost impossible standards.

Special thanks also to the many proof-readers involved in this project, including Stephen Amy, Tony Holler, David Pagard, Jeffery Price, Mick Tillman and especially the 7th graders at CSCS Woodland Park, including the author's daughter, Mary Holler, and her classmate Heidi Bacorn.

About the Author:

Mike Holler is an alumnus of both the Master's College and Biola University, where he studied literary interpretation and translation.

He lives with his wife Cathy and four of their seven children in the mountains of Colorado. Mike is a freelance writer and speaker, as well as a frequent guest and guest host on radio. He travels regularly with the Tea Party Express and is available to speak on the subject of the United States Constitution virtually anywhere in the United States.

Ordering and Inquiries:

For speaking engagements or other inquiries please contact the author directly via email: MikeHoller@aol.com.

Book discounts are available in quantity; as well as for educational, promotional, or premium use. For orders please visit TheConstitutionMadeEasy.com.

Have you ever wondered how legends came into being? Have you ever desired to learn from the legends of history? Have you ever desired to become a legend? 12 authors bring you stories of courage, mentorship & virtue through *Legends of Liberty*!

Legends of Liberty tells the story of 15 legends throughout history and teaches the reader how to emulate their actions in modern society. Each chapter is written by a different author, each a modern day legend in their own right.

Legends of Liberty is edited, compiled, and formulated by Rick Green. Contributing authors include David Barton, Gary Newell, Cliff Graham, Krish Dhanam, Timothy Barton, Brad Stine, Paul Tsika, Alexandra Murphy, and many others!

Legends and stories told include John Locke, King David, Nathan Hale, Squanto, Zig Zigler, Sybil Ludington, Brian Birdwell, Jimmy Robertson, Divey Langston, Moe Berg, and many others!

314

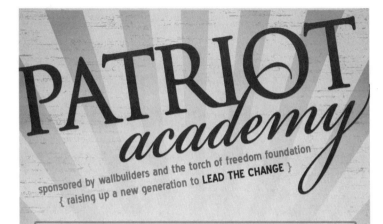

CHALLENGE YOUR IDEA OF GOVERNMENT

At Patriot Academy, you don't just learn about government, you live it. This summer, you and your fellow students, ages 16-25, will take over the Texas state government at the Capitol Building in Austin, Texas. You will work together to form a fully functioning mock government, drafting legislation, running committee meetings, debating bills, electing leaders and passing laws.

CONFRONT THE ISSUES OF TODAY

In a fast-paced, interactive format, elected officials and experts will explain today's most relevant issues. Through media relations training, public speaking workshops and spirited debate, you will learn to articulate what you believe and why. Patriot Academy will equip you to effect change for the issues that matter most to you, whether as a concerned citizen or political candidate.

CHAMPION THE CAUSE OF FREEDOM

If you want to be a part of a new generation of young leaders poised to change the future of American politics, join us at Patriot Academy. You won't want to miss it!

FOR MORE INFORMATION OR TO APPLY, VISIT US AT
WWW.PATRIOTACADEMY.COM

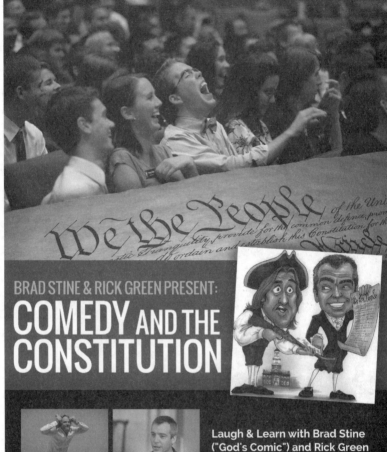

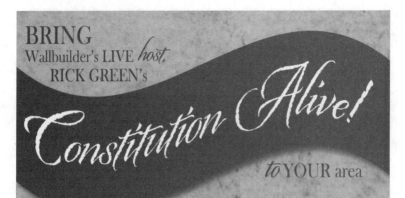

ABOUT THE AUTHOR...

Rick is a former Texas State Representative, attorney, author, and nationally recognized speaker on the Constitution and America's founding principles. He currently co-hosts the daily radio talk show ***WallBuilders Live! w/David Barton***. Rick and his wife, Kara, and their children travel the Nation together teaching on the Constitution and inspiring citizens to do their part in protecting our cherished freedoms. They bring history to life with their fun and entertaining adventures in their ***Chasing American Legends*** reality television series.

Connect with the Green family at RickGreen.com for regular updates, articles, and liberty inspiring information!